MORE THAN

*a*LIVING

WHAT CORPORATE INSIDERS DO TO ACHIEVE CAREER GROWTH, LEADERSHIP, AND PURPOSE

KATE SHATTUCK

More Than a Living:
What Corporate Insiders Do to Achieve Career Growth, Leadership, and Purpose
by Kate Shattuck

1. BUS037020 BUSINESS & ECONOMICS / Careers / Job Hunting
2. BUS012030 BUSINESS & ECONOMICS / Careers / Career Advancement & Professional Development
3. BUS056030 BUSINESS & ECONOMICS / Careers / Resumes

ISBN (hardcover): 979-8-88636-080-6
ISBN (paperback): 979-8-88636-081-3
ISBN (ebook): 979-8-88636-082-0

Library of Congress Control Number: 2026907097

Cover design by Lewis Agrell

Printed in the United States of America

Authority Publishing
13389 Folsom Blvd #300-256
Folsom, CA 95630
800-877-1097

www.AuthorityPublishing.com

"Brilliant. *More Than a Living* is more than a book! It is a profound and pragmatic navigation guide to a more fulfilling, purpose-filled life. Get this book, savor it, and nourish your unique contribution to the world."
– Kevin Cashman
Vice Chairman of Korn Ferry and bestselling author of
Leadership from the Inside Out and *The Pause Principle*

"*More Than a Living* is the kind of book every champion, mentor, and sponsor should place directly into the hands of the people they believe in. It's not just career guidance, it's a blueprint for leading a life of purpose, impact, and integrity.

If you are invested in someone's growth, give them this book. And honestly? Give it to your children, too. The lessons here don't just shape careers; they shape the humans we hope they will become."
– Barbara Morrison
Founder, TMC Financing

"Highly recommend. Learning from others, mistakes and all, ensures a smart, well-reasoned career strategy and a pathway to a more gratifying life. Kate Shattuck takes the reader there in a no-nonsense, demystifying, and entertaining career/life campaign. This book is needed now more than ever."
– Marc Patrick Cosentino
Author of *Case in Point*

"After more than 10,000 executive interviews, Kate Shattuck has seen firsthand what separates candidates who advance from those who stall. *More Than a Living* is a practical guide to understanding how hiring, promotion, and professional reputation really work."
– Tom Kent
CEO of CareerNerds and
author of *Executive Fast Track*

"I've admired Kate Shattuck's sharp insight since our time advising leaders at Korn Ferry, and this book is everything I hoped she'd write. Kate doesn't just tell you what to do; she tells the hard truth about why most people don't—with the kind of straight-talking, real-world guidance that cuts through the noise. If you're serious about building a rewarding career, not just holding down a job, this book is for you."
– Margie Warrell
PhD, global leadership speaker,
C-suite advisor, bestselling author
of *The Courage Gap*

"A brilliant, systematic strategy for people who want more than just a job. *More Than a Living* is the ultimate blueprint for turning life's pressure into both elite performance and profound personal fulfillment."

— Fran Lawler, CEO,
Harvest Cove Talent Partners

"As a Chief People Officer, I've participated in many interviews from entry-level team member to C-Suite. I wish every person I've interviewed could read this book! Kate provides both practical and tactical-level tips AND key emotional intelligence details that many don't consider. This is a fast-track guide on how to increase your chances to get selected at your next career progression opportunity! I recommend this book to our team members as they continue their own professional journey. Highly recommend!"

– Noble Gibbens
Chief People Officer of Kiefer Sage,
Podcast Host: EQ Gangster

"*More Than a Living* speaks directly to those who have built careers while also carrying the profound responsibility of caring for a wounded veteran. Kate Shattuck—herself a veteran, military spouse, and longtime champion for America's Hidden Heroes—captures the resilience, honesty, and purpose that define this community. Her insights offer caregivers and professionals alike a roadmap to grow, lead, and thrive without losing sight of the service and love that shape our lives."

— Steve Schwab, CEO,
Elizabeth Dole Foundation

More Than a Living is a candid, insider's guide to the realities of corporate life. Kate Shattuck offers the real, unfiltered truths that people need to hear. The book includes practical strategies every ambitious professional needs to accelerate their career and build a meaningful life. She is the corporate godmother you wish you had.

— Stephanie Rupp
Board Chair, US SIF,
Former CEO & Partner, Veris Wealth Partners

TABLE OF CONTENTS

Epigraph

"Having a vocation is something of a miracle,
like falling in love."

Admiral Hyman G. Rickover

Introduction

When I see a person who is genuinely happy with their job, their career, I see a person who is in love with their whole life.

Your job is not the most important thing, but it does affect your attitudes, your personal economic situation, and yes, it impacts your family's happiness too . . . who wants a grumpy person coming home? No one.

I also see a great number of people who want career advice and are searching for it on TikTok or LinkedIn videos. That's a place to start, but really? Do I want my next hire, my co-workers, mentees, and the next generation of leaders getting advice from someone in a hoodie posting from the front seat of their car? Don't you deserve better?

First off, no offense to those folks in hoodies. Much of that "casual" advice is actually good. But for it to provide you with any valuable guidance, you need more context and a little more time and attention.

This book is for you, an emerging leader. You might have a good job but want a career, you might want to climb the corporate ladder, you might want more pay, or to be able to make a bigger difference in the world. For sure, you want more out of your job. It's for the person with some work experience who realizes that the people who are getting ahead are playing a corporate game, and they don't know the rules.

Most importantly, this book is for you if you are willing to hear some hard truths, are open to doing things differently, and are committed to doing the necessary work to get ahead.

I wrote this book to share with you all the insider knowledge I've gained over 30 years of experience, and that includes the many mistakes I've made (and learned from). The truth is that I have lived through every one of the career challenges this book explores. Coming from a family background of modest means, I took full advantage of everything that was available to me: education, extra-curriculars, training, opportunities, mentors, champions, and yes, luck! Yet even after I earned an MBA from Harvard, I wish someone had told me some of the corporate truths that I only learned by having a seat at the executive tables where hiring and promotion decisions are made—behind closed doors. Over more than a decade as an executive recruiter, I have literally been part of 10,000 interviews with 10,000 highly qualified individuals. I advise CEOs and boards on their talent strategy, culture, and business. I have taken this knowledge to become not only a leader at Korn Ferry but also an investor in companies with great leaders, and both a nonprofit and public company board member. In this process, I learned a great deal about who gets the best jobs and why they succeed. I want you to understand what happens behind the scenes so you can be as prepared as possible.

Today, more than ever, the job market is full of uncertainty. Most people aren't in a position to "lean in." They are just trying to stay seated during the turbulence! Most people can't imagine taking no salary to start up a business. Most of us are looking for sound advice on how to not only survive, but maybe just a little, thrive by finding a job and a career that gives us a little joy.

The pace of change today is so fast that it's not easy to know what you want to do, but you know more about yourself than you think. On the cover of this book is a Great Horned Owl, a symbol of wisdom and knowledge. This book is an effort to show you—draw out of you—the self-knowledge and wisdom that you already have. And then, I know you can direct it into action in the real world, whether that is on Main Street or in a suburban office park or a big city high-rise.

I believe in you. You go get 'em.

~ 11 ~

Have you heard any good news lately? Mostly, the headlines are about a terrible job market, no job security, AI coming for millions of white-collar positions, and predictions that young adults entering the labor market are expected to have less financial success than their parents. Crushing student debt, starter homes priced out of reach, cost of living going up weekly. If you're struggling to launch or get promoted, it's easy to understand why.

I wrote this book to share some good news. You don't have to surrender to the doom and gloom. Of course, you can resign yourself to living in your parents' basement while staying on their Netflix and cell phone accounts forever; you can stay in your dead-end job and look forward to every day with a sense of dread. Or you can face up to some hard truths about what it takes to build a rewarding work life. With some insight and encouragement, you can start doing what it takes to find opportunity, even in these challenging times. I've been there and done that, so I know you can too.

Part One is all about tackling the massive problem of figuring out what you want to do, maybe not for your whole life, but for better and for now. Each chapter starts with a simple but often uncomfortable truth and ends with a hack, aka a skill to not only help you cope, but also step up a little, reach a little . . . grow. In between, you'll find explanations, examples, and the occasional story or two from my lived experience or those generously offered from my friends, clients, and candidates over the course of the last 30 years. Forget that tired and worthless advice to "follow your passion." Ignore the shallow "life advice" offered in a series of TikTok clips. With some savvy and awareness, you can navigate through this unfamiliar world where you are basically a tourist without Google Maps or Duolingo, venturing into corporate America. Now is your time to get real and get started. I'm here to help.

ONE
Your Career Belongs to You

If you're a recent grad or are new to full-time work, chances are the world seems chaotic, confusing, and out of control. Up to now, pretty much your whole life has had structure. You went to school, had weekends, holidays and summers off, and every year you got a "promotion" by moving up a grade level. You were given regular assignments, got grades and feedback on your work, and had a pretty good idea of where you ranked. But once that diploma landed in your hand, all that structure disappeared. No more semesters, no more spring break, no more summers off. No more assigned work, no more grades and counseling.

It's exciting to be free. But it's also like stepping into a great unknown. If our society was trying to design a way to set young adults up to fail, we couldn't have come up with a better system. Plan out every minute for 18 or 20 years, then take it all away. Suddenly, you're expected to start "adulting" and pay your own cell phone bill. Freedom. Identity crisis. Panic. Excitement! And, financial anxiety big time.

Maybe you were savvy enough to major in a field that helped you land your first job, or maybe you fell into it. Maybe you got a degree in something you discovered you didn't especially like, and the thought of being stuck in that career fills you with dread. Or maybe you breezed through high

**The Hard Truth/
What Insiders Know**

You alone are 100% responsible for building your career.

school or college without giving much thought to the skills you might need to find rewarding work. Suddenly, everyone is asking you what you're going to do with your life, and you have no clue. You can't undo the past, but you can take charge of the present.

You Are Not a Special Lump of Clay

My first work crisis came when I was fresh out of a stint in the military. I'd landed a great job in my chosen field, in a company I really liked. In my mind, I was this awesome lump of precious golden clay, full of energy and experience, ready to be molded and shaped by my employer into the next wonderkid investor, CEO, head of sales . . . whatever they needed me to be. I was very willing to describe all the ways in which I was amazing, but I had no idea what specific value I brought to the company. I was looking for my employer to tell me what they saw in me. Naively, I thought if I just showed up and said what I'm good at, someone would tell me how I fit into their company.

I should have been concentrating on what they needed as a company and thinking about how I could be a part of their strategy. It was up to me to do the doing: figure out how, day to day, I could advance the company's business. It began to dawn on me that what I did in school and in the military was far less important than the results and performance I could deliver *today*.

When I began to realize it was up to me to figure out who I was, what I needed from a job or workplace, and what *value* I could bring to an employer, it put me in a different mindset. What I now call extreme ownership. No one was interested in shaping and molding me. And I was lucky, there was a new employee training program, and there was formal and informal mentorship. But no one was dedicated—really focused—on investing the time and effort into helping me figure out what I could and should be doing. The only decision anyone was going to make for me was deciding I wasn't a "good fit" for their company.

It's not that nobody cares exactly, but nobody cares enough to take you on as a project when they already have more than enough to do with work, family, and life. I had to accept that I am fully responsible for making my way in the world. The world does not owe me anything. I have to earn whatever satisfaction and success I'm going to achieve.

On your first day as a new hire, you may feel very important. You have a workstation, a new computer, and the boss takes you around to introduce you to the team. You're the brand-new butterfly, flitting around, attracting attention. But day two (or after lunch!), it's up to you to start showing that you're there to benefit the company and its clients. The sooner you figure out what that means, how things work, how decisions get made and who makes them, the faster you'll find success. You have to learn that your boss and other team members have KPIs: key performance indicators or metrics on their performance. And these are tied to how they are paid. And guess what: you do too! The company wants you to succeed, but they're not going to do the work for you. Companies can be empathetic—they might pick you up if you trip and fall, but ultimately, they care about themselves more than they care about you.

Make Real Connections

"No one cares" sounds harsh, but it's true, with one saving grace. You can build a community that cares and will support you. And having a supportive community is far more effective and rewarding than trying to go it alone. Find some people who are willing to invest their time in you because you can help them meet their goals. These might be financial, personal, or professional. Don't be super exclusive and stay in only one type of community of people just like you. When I was in the Army, for instance, I chose to live off base so I could interact with non-military people. Ideally, whatever group you join should offer some diversity while still being made up of people who care about you and not your job title. If you're already working, look for informal opportunities to spend time getting to know people from work. Be on the lookout for mentors. There are often more senior professionals who want to stay current and value your fresh perspectives. You provide your unique point of view, and they share what experience has taught them.

Especially in a post-COVID world, building a real face-to-face, live-time community might seem daunting. But it is easier and more fun than you fear. It doesn't matter if you're joining a work team or a softball team; the basics of integration are the same. A smile goes a long way. Try out easy ways to start the conversation, for instance, "I'm Sam, and I'm new here. How long have you worked here?"

Look for professional or affinity associations in your community or within the company, groups such as women entrepreneurs, a kickball team, or a college alumni association. Ask lots of questions, but not in an annoying way. Listen to the answers. Volunteer. Join the clean-up crew after meetings and events, when people have more time and are more open to chatting. Word gets around that you are doing more than the minimum and showing that you want to belong.

Set yourself the goal to cultivate three areas, or buckets, of meaningful activity: professional, personal, and community. Be a part of some group or entity that is larger than you. Actively work at building relationships that nourish you. Create a community that is there when you need support and one where you can support others. But it is still up to you to do the work.

Tree vs. Landscape

When you're getting started, the first challenge is to figure out what you want to do. Instead of stressing over deciding once and for all on your career, think of your first series of jobs as the chance to find out more about yourself.

What do I like/need in the workplace? What am I good at?

What type of environment makes me most comfortable and productive? How much time am I willing to commit to work? Keep experimenting to find the right combination of elements. Look for the work/life/environment that makes you feel the best. No one is going to do this assessment for you. In fact, no one can do this for you. You can make a poor choice, fail, assess, improve, reassess, and recover. Each move doesn't have to be the "final, final" revised version.

You may spend years moving from job to job, looking for the right everything. And let's face it, there are plenty of times when what you have to have is a job that pays the bills, keeps food on the table, and a roof over your head. But endless job hopping won't magically become a career. Job hopping—moving companies every few months or every year or so—usually means a short-term bump in pay or running away from a bad boss, but without real professional growth or increased satisfaction.

Having a career, instead of a job, is actually a privilege. A career is more of a long game—being able to make moves that help you grow, give back to your community and world. You might "happen" into a career, but not if you don't pay attention to opportunity. Careers have an element of development in them. You grow into expertise, passing markers of mastery and maturity until you have accomplished enough to have special and unique experience and value to deliver to the company. Building a career gives you the opportunity to achieve excellence and to become a subject matter expert. This level of mastery can connect you to a higher purpose, giving you satisfaction in a job well done. This doesn't have to mean "getting to the top" or being the CEO or a mega popstar. It means doing work that adds significance to the company, to your community, and provides real gratification and meaning to you.

Along the way you are bound to have doubts about what to do next. How do I know what is a great opportunity and what is a dead end? You're not alone. You don't have to know all the steps ahead. It's a journey that is built on jobs well done, not on random job hopping. And spoiler alert, it won't be amazing all the time. Sometimes it's a frustrating, exhausting slog. But when you get through it, you've learned or earned something worthwhile. Building a career means working to de-risk your situation by being keenly aware of how you are adding value. What that also translates into is providing some protection against inevitable downturns, making you less likely to be laid off, downsized, or even replaced by AI.

**Helpful Hack/
What Insiders Do**

Join one professional or social organization.

Make a list of what you are good at and enjoy doing.

I've come to think of a career as a series of jobs with a throughline that helps develop unique expertise. It's a landscape instead of a single tree. And just as a landscape has hills and valleys, peaks and troughs, days of sunshine and rain, your career will include all those ups and downs.

TWO
Find the Right Work

You've got your eye on what looks like a cool job. Flexible hours, decent pay, maybe even a hip company culture, and cool merch. Ticks a lot of boxes for you, but there's one big problem: It's a sales job, and you have never worked in sales (or worse, you don't actually like people). Here's where many of us feel like we've run into a wall too high to climb. How can I get the experience companies are looking for when no one will hire me? Want a leg up? Read on.

Where to Start Looking?

(Spoiler alert: Not on an online job board.)

Finding the work that's right for you starts with you taking the initiative. There are four distinct phases in a focused job search designed to get you to a solid interview. In this chapter, we're going to break down the first two. The others we'll cover later. Here they are.

- Phase One. Understand who you are by examining your experience so far.
- Phase Two. Learn about what it's like to work in various industries and fill your experience gaps.
- Phase Three. Understand the

**The Hard Truth/
What Insiders Know**

Experience is a great teacher.

market and create your personal brand.
- Phase Four. Build a network and "work your network" to get closer to the decision makers.

Phase One: As a Job Seeker, Who Am I?

Understanding who you are as an employee starts with looking at how you have thrived or died in various environments. In chapter one, you listed things you are both good at and enjoy doing. Now turn those insights into three adjectives that most fully and honestly describe you.

It helps to ask yourself a lot of questions to find your adjectives:

- Who are you when you're at your very best?
- How would your co-workers describe you?
- How would your supervisor describe you?
- What would your customers say about you?

Think of these adjectives less as being about emotion and more about skill. Please don't say, "I'm a people person." It's nice to care about people, but how does that make you better at your job? You're not going to get hired for your personality alone, but your personality translates a lot into the skills and abilities you bring to the company.

I can't stress enough that those three adjectives have to be really true to you. You have to believe them in your heart, because otherwise you will not be able to communicate convincingly who you are. You won't be able to show the value in who you are.

And who you are goes beyond your skills and abilities. It also has to include your current wants and needs. What do I need at this moment in my life? Do I want a title? Do I want money? Do I want to work with great people? Do I want to work at a brand that my mother knows? Is it about my commute to work because I have kids? Do I crave complex challenges? Do I want something less demanding because I already have a lot to balance in my life?

The answers to these questions are for you, not for your parents, your partner, or your peers. As you start looking for work, you have to really know what you need and want from a job now. It's ok to say "money" because we all need it. Maybe you need a job while you're getting a degree. Maybe you plan to move into your own apartment and are saving money. Maybe you want to find a company you can stay with for years. You may even be asking yourself, "Is this a job that will lead me to my eventual best job ever?'

Knowing who you are, what you enjoy, what you need, what you're good at, and what you think you'd like to do saves you from chasing jobs that won't work out. In the wrong job or the wrong company, you'll be bored, stressed, frustrated, and probably underachieving because it's not a good fit for who you are.

Phase Two: Explore the Field

Let's look at the experience gap you may think is holding you back. A good place to start is by learning about the industries or careers you are interested in pursuing. What specific skills do they look for in an employee? There's no better way to know this than by talking to people who do the jobs you find appealing.

It might be hard to think about reaching out blind to a whole industry. So, first, start with those closest to you. Think about family friends or relatives in different occupations who may be willing to help you. Think about roommates, friends and their parents, siblings, and community groups. Another way to find folks to interview is by going to job fairs. You're not here to sell yourself. You're here to gather information from the people who work for this company.

This doesn't have to be scary. If you give people the chance to talk about themselves and what they do, unless they hate their jobs (which is valuable intel!), people enjoy talking about their work. It's helpful to have a set of questions you want to ask: Tell me about how you got this job. What's your typical day like? What's the best part of your job? What is the hardest part? What are your success metrics (or what are your key performance indicators)? What do you love about your job? What do you hate about your job? And here's a big one: How do you get paid? You're not asking them to disclose their salary. You're trying to understand how compensation works in their industry. Is it on a commission basis? Bonus incentives? Pay grades tied to titles? Annual pay raises tied to the cost of living?

It's almost like the story about the blind people and the elephant. You're feeling your way, getting information to help you form a picture of the whole animal. Each conversation you have adds more detail. This is the ear of the elephant, this is a leg, the tail, and so on. You have to really, really be curious.

These conversations use direct questions to help you decide if this sounds like a job in a company where you'd be a good fit—or even if the industry really does interest you. You might compare it to going into a dressing room to try on clothes. On the rack, you thought this looked great, but now you have some decisions to make. How does this color suit you? Is this outfit too tight or too loose? Are you willing to invest in alterations, or is this good enough? Is it more important to wear something that is on trend, or something that looks and feels right for you? This may seem silly, but too often job seekers aren't asking themselves the right questions before firing off hundreds of applications. It's up to you to figure out where you fit in the job market. If you're going to apply randomly to hundreds of job postings, you're going to lose. You're going to get stuck in the algorithm of the application process and waste your time going down dead ends (to say nothing of how discouraging and depressing that feels, like wearing something truly awful!). You have to think about yourself as the product, but you're also the marketer. It takes an investment of your time and maybe even investing in more training, experience, and networking. But until you do this work to get clarity on what you want and what you bring to the workplace, you're not even ready to *apply* for a job. And you surely are not ready to interview.

Phase Three: Find and Fill the Gaps

Your goal is to identify maybe three to five companies you want to apply to, and some specific positions that seem both attractive and attainable. You may not have the identical *experience* these positions require, but do you have the *skills?* If not now, how can you fill the skills gaps? You might need a professional certificate or license. Maybe you have to get an advanced degree, but probably not. There might be a volunteer opportunity at your current company or at a community organization where you could fill the gap in that knowledge, skill, or ability, so you can show you've earned it. Or there may be something in your past experience that demonstrates that you have the necessary skill. You have to showcase it.

This process, by the way, will happen again and again during your career. It's not just for first-time job seekers. A friend of mine was retiring from the military with twenty years of work experience, but she wanted to pivot to a role in business development for a defense company. Her resume was impressive except that she had zero sales experience. So she volunteered to be a fundraiser and find sponsors for her kid's school silent auction. This was a modest commitment that was also a test. She was going to find out not only if she could do the outreach and handle the rejection of sales, but also if she was good at it and enjoyed it. She believed in the mission of raising funds for her kid's school, and she was willing to put herself out there to sell sponsorships. As it turns out, she loved the work, and she was quite good at it. That gave her confidence and some proof she could offer at her interview.

If you want a job in financial services, for example, you could try making up your own internship. Actively manage your personal finances, maybe within your current 401k or modest retirement account. If you don't have an investment account, take part in a contest on Yahoo Finance or other organizations that have contests where you can pick stocks over a period of time.

If you're interested in an operations or customer service job, how can you find the value in your role as a Starbucks barista? Were you able to suggest ways to make the operation more efficient? Did you find ways to make the customer experience more interesting? Did you figure out what kind of customer interactions earned a tip? What kind didn't? All of these things are useful ways to show you do have experience. They are tangible examples that show how you, today, are actively engaged in making the work and the customer experience better. Even if it's one cup at a time, you are able to deliver different kinds of enhanced value for your company.

I'm sharing these examples to suggest that with some creativity, you can manufacture your own experience. Then, when you finally go into that interview, you can say with conviction, "I have this relevant experience, and it shows what I am capable of doing."

Phase Four: Your Command Message

Focus on two or three really great things that you've done at your current job, for your project team, or volunteer organization. What are your big successes? Have you been Employee of the Month, beat your sales target, had a breakthrough idea, come up with a way to improve job efficiency or customer satisfaction, or simply been the person everyone wants to work with? Being able to answer the question about where you have been successful puts you on a path to identifying how your personality, skills, and strengths combine for the greatest impact. These are also the examples you need to share when you are proving you are, and who you claim to be. You are someone who delivers results!

You have to know these answers so you can convey what we call in the military a command message. You may know it as an elevator speech, but I prefer the authority—and confidence—of calling it a command message. Once you know your three adjectives, you can back them up with examples of the things you're really good at. You then understand how these match what the employer is looking for, and this yields the necessary ingredients for an attention-getting command message: This is who I am, and this is what I can do for you.

A strong command message is short, easily understood, powerful, and unable to be ignored, just like a command. It sounds like this, "I'm a leader who gets results. My team came in first place even though we were the least experienced group in the contest," or "I'm a risk taker who suggested three new services that added new sources of sales," or "I'm a straight talker, and I give people feedback they can receive that helps amplify their performance."

Giddy Up: Start Logging Your 10,000 Hours

In Malcolm Gladwell's book, *Outliers*, he famously advanced the concept that it takes 10,000 hours of dedicated work to achieve genuine mastery of any skill. At three hours a day, it would take more than nine years of real effort. So please, while I want you to celebrate the wins and skills your experience so far has earned you, be humble. You're more than a "special lump of clay," but you're not capable of running the show. Not yet.

Employers often hire for potential. They are looking for people who have skills and are willing to learn more and go beyond. In my line of work, executive recruiting, new recruiters make tons of phone calls. They send a lot of emails. In every outreach to a new candidate, they get better. They experiment. They see which emails get traction. They decide if a phone call, an email, or a text is more effective. They try sending a message through LinkedIn. All of these are experiments and practice to help them get better at their first goal, getting a potential candidate to respond. Believe me, their supervisors pay attention to who is experimenting, risking rejection, applying what they learn, and gaining expertise in their job.

When I was growing up, my dad sold cars. At first, he was good at it, but not great. But he liked it and was interested in getting better. He volunteered to take extra shifts. He offered to deal with "bad" customers that no one else wanted. Sometimes, on the weekends, he would drive to another car dealership 100 miles away and pretend to be a customer. He would go through the sales process to see how other salesmen went about trying to sell to him. He learned a lot about what works and what doesn't. One time, on one of these adventures to another dealership, he had a woman salesperson, and he told me she was so good that he nearly bought a car we did not need! Instead, he gave her $100 and thanked her for the great sales lesson. My dad built himself up to be a very successful salesman after having a lot of starts and stops in other careers. But when he found car sales, he was a natural at it, and he worked to get better all the time. After five years, he was a master. It was as if he really grew up. He was able to establish mastery in a craft that not only paid him, but also gave him confidence and pride.

No matter what your job is, if you want to move ahead in your career, you have to commit to practicing your craft. Experience is a great teacher, so keep getting new experiences. Start logging those 10,000 hours with openness and purpose.

Helpful Hack/ What Insiders Do

Make a list and contact 6–10 people to talk to about their jobs.

Write your command message (use AI only if you must).

Next Up

Once you've completed Phases One and Two, you're ready to tackle the next challenge: How do I want to be seen? The next chapter is all about learning to market yourself.

THREE
Becoming Your Own
Chief Marketing Officer

You might think a first impression forms the moment you walk through the door for your interview. It used to be like that, pre-Internet and social media, but not today. Now it's routine for employers to find you online, check out your socials, and use what they see as a way to sort out if you're worth considering. This is, of course, if your resume has made it through the chatbot algorithm.

You've made it to the top of the resume pile for a position you really want. Don't blow it by accidentally or carelessly sending the wrong message about who you are. It's complicated. Even with AI screening resumes, we are still human beings, and no human being is strictly one-dimensional. Nobody wants to be flat Andy. We interact differently with family, with friends, with co-workers, and with strangers. You want to be seen. But by whom and in what way? For a serious job/career seeker, it's crucial to learn how to be your own chief marketing officer (CMO). No one can do this for you, although you can and should get some sound advice. That's what this chapter delivers.

How Do You Want to Show Up?

Let's begin by stressing the importance of being authentic. Whatever image you project has to be real. A company

**The Hard Truth/
What Insiders Know**

You only get one shot at a first impression.

might hire a fake, but they won't keep them. People can smell an impostor. So how do you go about identifying who you are at your most essential? And how can you communicate that message consistently, honestly, and genuinely?

Go back to the exercise in chapter two that asked you for three adjectives to describe yourself. Are they words that make you feel good about yourself, feel true to who you are, and reflect what others would say about you? Maybe people you work with have other adjectives for you, or the folks on your softball team, or your friends from college. There are going to be differences. Don't try to hide an alternative life. If you love competitive volleyball, it's fine to own it. What you want to look for are the things that are constant and true and would show up in your 9–5 work life.

Fun, honest, a sports nut, direct, passionate, energetic, thoughtful, reliable, hilarious. Even though the people in the different parts of your life might describe you in different ways, are there some words they share in common? Generate a list of at least 10 positive ones to emphasize and help shape your image. From that list, can you find three traits that everyone who knows you sees and recognizes? This is how you want to appear online and in person. Basically, you don't want anyone to put you in a box you don't want to be in. Find the box that is the best fit for you now.

"Now" is important because your image can and should change over time. Who you were in high school shouldn't be exactly who you still are at 25. And it's equally important to realize who you are, and how people see you, is up to you.

Your Image is a Precious Asset

When I was a West Point cadet, rebellious was my middle name. I was struggling as a young adult to figure out how to be part of a disciplined, rigid system while still remaining myself. My solution was to act out, defy the rules, and pretty much be a pain in the ass. Then one day, I figured out that if I wanted to be a leader in the military, able to give orders and not just follow them, being a rebel was not going to get me there. No one was going to let my rule breaking self be responsible for America's sons and daughters. I set about changing my behavior to show (not only the Army, but myself) that not only could I lead, I could be a great officer. First, I had to be a good example. I also realized that my own rebellious past helped me understand and manage the rebelliousness in other young recruits.

Years later, my CO (commanding officer) met someone who had been at West Point with me. He asked him what I had been like in school and was shocked to hear me described as "crazy, wild, and a big partier." Those were not words my CO would ever have attached to me now. I was proud to hear this story because it showed that reputations can be repaired and actions can be redirected without giving up who you are. It showed me that reputations are assets, like owning a home or a retirement savings account. My reputation went from damaging to valuable, and yours can too.

When you are applying for a job, do some research on what the company culture and its values appear to be. Do they look for innovation or scrupulous following of procedures? Is it an "anything goes" culture where you see employees with all kinds of fashion and dress, or is it white shirts and blue blazers? You can figure this out from the image the company projects on their website and socials, and even better, what the employees are posting. Your challenge is to decide if you can meet their expectations and blend in to their world without losing the really important parts of who you are. Also, is this a brand that you WANT TO blend into? If yes, then build an authentic image that makes you as irresistible as Reese's Peanut Butter Cups at Halloween or Bud Light on the 4th of July. You want to be the product that sells from the supermarket end cap displays, a must-have choice.

A Stranger in Corporate America

Especially when you are starting out in your professional work life, the workplace can seem as baffling as landing in a foreign country where no one speaks English. It takes time and paying attention to navigate your way through this unfamiliar territory. It's not as if swiping right on profiles of senior execs in the company, or voting "hot or not," is going to advance your career.

Once you're in, you still have to be mindful and intentional about your image. Pay attention to what people say about you. Try to figure out what they think about you. Your supervisor will do this during your periodic reviews, either formally every year or informally on a more regular basis. Pay attention to the adjectives they use. Same with your peers. Even if your company doesn't have a formal peer (sometimes referred to as 360-degree feedback) review process, ask your co-workers for an informal check-in and listen to what they say.

Marketing yourself within the company never ends if you want to keep growing and achieving. Carla Harris, a legendary corporate leader in the male-dominated finance industry, tells a story about her own internal marketing campaign. In a performance review that praised her results, Harris was also told that she was perceived as "too nice" to get a promotion. You can write this off as being gender biased, but Harris was determined to rewrite the script. Every time she assigned a project to anyone on her team, she ended with the caution, "I'm going to check over your work, and you know I'm really tough." It wasn't as if her standards or her behavior toward co-workers had changed. What was different was that she was explicitly describing herself as tough. Months later, she overheard two junior execs talking about their project and reminding each other that it had to be 100% because "Harris is really tough." Victory!

How do you want to be known? The answer will help you decide where you want to invest more time and effort. What is the result you want from the time you put in at work? Often that means volunteering for specific assignments or informal company teams, like offering to help a stressed co-worker without demanding credit, running the March Madness pool (but only if you are truly into college hoops), or the Halloween party. I had a co-worker who ran the office pool for March Madness. As a junior account manager, he quickly got to know every senior exec in the company. It was a smart way to get the right kind of attention to build your image—because of the visibility and because he was passionate about college basketball. Doesn't it sound worth the extra effort if co-workers start thinking of you as a great colleague who is always there for them?

Dress for Success

Yes, it's a catchy cliché, but it is still true. We can't help ourselves. We all judge by appearances first, interactions second. I knew a man who was an undercover agent for the FBI. On his own time, he was a devoted biker who dressed the part: black leather everything, chains as accessories, etc. Surprise. Every time he went through airport security in his personal wardrobe, he got pulled out for an interview. He finally figured out this was not the best situation for an undercover agent, so he began wearing button-down shirts and a navy blue blazer when flying. Problem solved. No extra security checks.

So, before you start applying for real jobs, scrub some of those socials. Tank tops and tats? Goofy selfies? You're not in a cool contest. You want to be taken seriously for the person with talent and ambition you are. Get a professional headshot or at least take the picture of you and your puppy off your LinkedIn profile. LinkedIn is the new business card, so it matters.

Helpful Hack/ What Insiders Do

Much of this will be new to you. Start trying on your image like you would some clothes. How does it feel? How do you look to yourself?

And while you're at it, buy some professional clothes and get used to wearing them.

Update your LinkedIn headshot with a more professional image—definitely no pets.

Start putting together a wardrobe that looks at home with how you see people dressed on the company website you're applying to. You don't have to spend a bundle on fancy clothes, and you don't have to change who you are, but you do have to pay attention to the image you are projecting. Ask yourself honestly, "Is this the image I want?"

Pro tip: Clothes that fit well are more impressive than designer tags. When I was applying for finance jobs in New York City, I shopped at consignment stores where I could get designer label hand-me-downs for a few dollars. Then I spent the money on a tailor to get the right fit. Having a good suit with a great fit made me feel like the million bucks I didn't have. Did the suit get me the job? Well, it didn't hurt. Decades later, I still have that suit because it symbolizes part of my image: my thriftiness, my freedom from financial need, and my gratitude to the tailor. If you dress like a boss, people will treat you like one.

FOUR
Acing the Interview

If an employer invites you to interview, even if the first round is over Zoom, it's a solid sign you are absolutely qualified for the job. No company wastes precious time interviewing also-rans or wannabes. That's the good news. Getting that first invitation should boost your confidence and put a big smile on your face. I want to celebrate that moment with you. So let's fist bump and then get started preparing.

Here's something the military teaches you. In moments of high stress or crisis, people do not rise to the occasion. They default to their highest level of training. You need to train yourself how to interview effectively. This is no time for winging it or hoping for the best. Interviews for corporate positions typically follow a predictable, consistent structure. At the beginning, there is a period of establishing rapport or getting to know each other, which is about 10 percent of the interview. Seventy percent of the time, you're going to be asked a series of questions, leaving you with about 20 percent of the time to ask your questions.

We'll look at each element of the interview process with suggestions for how to show up as your best self through these five stages: introduction, storytelling, strengths/weaknesses, your questions, and thank you.

The Hard Truth/ What Insiders Know

It's much harder to tell a short story than a long one.

Advance Prep

You've got your professional look sorted, with the right clothes, shoes, hair, makeup, and overall presentation in place, feeling comfortable. You don't want to be fidgeting with a collar, adjusting a neckline, or pushing back unruly hair. Nothing about your physical appearance should distract from what you are saying in an interview. Add a nice notebook and pen to your wardrobe. You'll want to be able to take notes, and a laptop or phone is too disruptive.

Study the job description carefully. Organizations often present a long list of qualifications they are seeking. To uncover what they consider most important, look at what they list first, second, and third, with the rest in descending order. You may also see the phrases "must have" or "demonstrable results" in the descriptions, so clearly, these are very important. You can't know for sure, but this gets you in the right direction. They saw something in your background that makes you a good fit. Now it's up to you to identify two or three essential skills that you convincingly have. These should map directly to the expectations for what that position is expected to accomplish. Go back to your command message and rework it to include these key skills. Practice delivering your message in a sentence or two.

You're about to enter the high-stakes world of interviewing. If you think of it like playing your favorite video game, it might seem more like a fun challenge than a paralyzing test. Once you're in the game, you'll use your skill to move to the next level. Game on.

Stage One: The Introduction

Generally, whether in person or online, every interview begins with the hiring manager, recruiter, or human resources staffer introducing themselves. They will probably tell you their title, describe their role, possibly offer a recap about the job, and provide some encouragement like, "We're really excited you've applied for the sales role."

Before you launch into your introduction, take a moment to ask the interviewer if they can go deeper into the job description. You want to assure them you're very familiar with the job posting, but you'd appreciate hearing more details. One way I've seen great candidates gather key intelligence at this early stage is to ask the interviewer if they can "breathe some life into the job description. What are the most important elements you are looking for?"

Take notes! You don't need a complete transcript. Just jot down words or phrases that suggest the specific skills, abilities, or traits they mention. These are your cues to address these important points when you talk about yourself and your experiences.

The interviewer is likely to give you an opening by asking, "Tell me a bit about yourself." This is where you breathe life into your command message. These first couple of sentences are really important. They don't want to hear a rambling recap of your resume and cover letter. They've already seen those. What they're looking for is a brief highlights reel: your accomplishments and expertise in three minutes or less. If your introduction takes five minutes, it's an epic fail.

Aim for a direct opening line that hits on your defining adjectives like, "I am a customer service-oriented manufacturing enthusiast." Bonus points if you can say it with a smile, even over the phone. Give an example that backs up your claim, and now you're the one breathing life into your resume. This first question is the proverbial softball . . . you can hit it out of the park.

Honestly, it took me a long time to find my short story. Like many of us, I think my background is so fabulous and interesting that I could talk about it for hours. But we're not at happy hour. In an interview, you have minutes, not hours. Especially if you're reiterating the jobs on your resume, people stop listening. They're signing a permission slip for their kid's field trip or checking their calendar. TikTok-er, you know people have a short attention span. Keep your message brief, clear, and—yes—interesting!

Have some fun practicing your introduction. You can video yourself, but it's even more effective if you deliver it to a real person. When I was a nervous job seeker about to graduate from business school, I practiced introducing myself to anyone who would listen. A bus driver, a cab driver, a random person on the subway. It was low risk because if I flubbed it, I was never going to see these people again. Everyone could tell how insecure I was, and every time they were so nice. The more I practiced, the more confident I became. I worked on getting the right tone of voice to sound natural instead of the wide pendulum of insecure to cocky or worse, robotic. Crafting a strong introduction was an effective weapon against nerves and helped me project ease and calmness. Your first few sentences set the interview tone for everything that comes next. Start strong, and the rest is much easier.

Remember, the introduction is not your green light to talk incessantly. Toss the mic back to your interviewer with a softball lob like, "Can you tell me more about you, too? How did you come to work at this company?" Take notes so you're set to level up in the game.

Stage Two:
Examples Through Storytelling (Show versus Tell)

The best preparation for an interview starts with anticipating the interviewer's questions. You can do a Google search to find the five to ten standard questions interviewers ask. Figure out how to answer each of these convincingly. Then look for proof of your claims in your background.

Do a careful reading of the job description to figure out what you think are the two or three most important skills required. Don't try to nail all 10. Next, think of some stories that provide examples of your relevant experience. If it's an operations job about making an office more efficient, the interviewer is bound to ask you about a time you made an office more efficient. If it's a sales job, they will ask about sales successes. The interviewer is a real person, trying to be highly efficient, so they often will start with the job description and turn it into questions.

If it's early in your career, you may not have many work examples, but look for something from your personal, academic, or volunteer life. Everybody has times when they've overcome challenges or faced down something hard. Your story should contain three elements: the circumstance, the action you took, and the result. One or two sentences per section, distilled into a simple story.

The way you lock in an image of yourself is by answering the question and telling a story. For a sales job, it could be something like this: "I was given a sales territory in southern Ohio where my company wanted to expand its retail (the circumstance). I visited every Lowe's, Home Depot, and mom-and-pop appliance distributor in the region and found out they all wanted bolder colors, like jewel tones and richer neutrals, instead of stainless steel. I took the data with a customer focus group to management, and that convinced my company to offer a moss green line (the actions taken). I then took samples to expos and grew sales by 49% (the result)."

By being specific, you've put a sharp picture in their mind that shows your initiative, determination, and impact. As Daniel Kahneman's book, *"Thinking Fast & Slow,"* and Michael Lewis's *"The Undoing Project"* have demonstrated, implicit bias affects our decision-making. Creating an image and story that sticks in someone's mind is a powerful way to use implicit bias to your advantage.

Stage Three:
Strengths and Weaknesses

Generally, it's easier for us to talk about our strengths and harder to admit to weaknesses. But be careful. Your strengths, overused, can be your weaknesses. You can be so collaborative that you don't make decisions. You can be so detail-oriented that you get bogged down and can't move to action. You can be so independent that you can be seen as aloof. Try linking each of your strengths directly to how they will make you successful in this role for this company. This level of detail shows you have not only studied the job description, but you also know something about the company culture, values, and overall mission. Is teamwork prized more than individual achievement? Is innovation at the core of the company's success? Is it important to be able to commit to long hours and lots of travel? Bonus points if there is something about your strengths that is forward-looking. For example, "I'm not afraid of tackling something new or of asking questions to help me find solutions."

When it comes to weaknesses, let's start with what to absolutely, positively, under no circumstances ever say. A weakness is not "I work too hard" or "I care too much." These are indicators that you don't know yourself.

The interviewer is actually less interested in the specifics of your answer than in what it reveals about how self-aware and mature you are. Do you have an ounce of humility? Have you done any honest reflecting on what you're good at and what you're not? Of course, you have a real weakness. Don't invent a fake one. It's important to be able to name it and describe how it shows up at work or even at home. It's the same storytelling approach: circumstance, action taken, result.

Keep in mind you're not going into therapy with this person, so make sure what you divulge is a professional weakness. And be sure to include how you deal with it so that it will help you in the role you're seeking. Tell your interviewer, "This is what I've done about my weakness to prevent it from causing a horrible failure."

What if, for instance, you're someone who likes reading and writing more than math? You could say, "I'm not great at math," and explain that you'd rather write a project report than do an Excel spreadsheet. But don't leave it there as a big, fat weakness. "I actually like manipulating formulas. When I have a task in Excel, I value having a teammate who can work with me or nudge me to get the spreadsheet completed."

Someone who is shy or lacking in personal confidence could

say "I'm a bit of an introvert." If they stopped there, there'd be a spotlight on the weakness. If they go on to say, "I realized I can do the necessary presentations to close inside sales, but I need to schedule some time to recover from the extra effort. That usually means relaxing after work with a cup of tea and my favorite crime novel." They've shown how they overcame the weakness.

These examples offer transparency and vulnerability, but most importantly, they show that you can solve for whatever weakness you know you have.

Record yourself talking through your strengths, weaknesses, and examples. Listen back so you can catch your own "umms" and "ahs" and practice until your delivery is conversational. The interviewing manager is a busy person. You have to be memorable in a positive way, so she advances you to the next level.

Stage Four: Your Questions

Wow. You're amazing. You've done a fabulous job fielding all the questions, and now it's your turn. Don't blow it by asking the worst possible question: "How much does the job pay?" There's a time for this inquiry, but it should not be your first question. We'll take a closer look at compensation and negotiation in the next chapter. For now, use your questions to go deeper into the specifics of the job and expectations.

You are trying to impress them with how interested you are in the job. Having questions ready in advance indicates interest and initiative. You're showing that you're thinking critically about whether this job is a good fit for you. Keep in mind, you are already qualified. Showing up with thoughtful questions puts you far ahead of most candidates who come prepared to answer questions but not to ask them.

One revealing question is, "In one year, what do you expect the person in this role to accomplish?" Another way to probe is to ask, "What is the one key metric this person will be judged on at 3, 6, 9, and 12 months?" These questions uncover more about the expectations for the job and give you more material to decide if it's a good fit for you. Does this work interest me? Is this a challenge worth taking? Are these guys crazy to expect such dramatic results? That's a red flag unless you enjoy taking on insanely unrealistic goals.

Stage Five: Thank You

An easy way to stand out is by saying thank you. Sending a note endears you to the interviewer, and in the age of the abbreviated text message, a genuine thank you, sent within twenty-four hours, sets you apart from your peers. An email sent quickly is acceptable, but a legible handwritten note sent by snail mail gets you a gold star. "Thank you so much for your time. I really appreciated getting to know more about your company. Have a great weekend. Sincerely, X." No need to overthink or overdo it.

Even if you don't think you'll get the job or your interview was a disaster, thank your interviewer. That positive final impression may earn you future consideration for another job.

If you haven't heard anything back after a week, it's fine to send an email inquiry like, "Thanks for spending time with me. Are there any updates on this role? I left our meeting excited to learn more, and I hope to hear back from you." If another week goes by, it's ok to send a fresh email with a new subject line. If you haven't heard back in 3 weeks, they have probably moved on, and you should too.

Then there's the awkward moment of getting a rejection phone call. The most professional companies, hiring managers, and recruiters try to contact you personally, but sometimes it's an email or voice mail. Remember to play the long game: even when you're being rejected, you are being evaluated for future potential. Not

Helpful Hack/ What Insiders Do

Prepare, practice, refine, and improve.

There is no such thing as over-preparing.

Make sure you have thoughtful questions ready in advance. Send a thank-you note.

right for this job at this time? It sucks. Still, be as professional as possible. Draw on every positive bone in your body while you say, "I'm disappointed, but I wish you well and thank you for calling me." It's fine to register disappointment, but end positively, "I hope someday we get a chance to work together." Recruiters and HR managers come back to candidates who leave a positive impression, so how you take a turndown is really important.

You can try to find out why you weren't chosen, but nowadays, companies are more risk-averse. The person you are speaking with might not really know why you weren't chosen, or they don't want to say something that (at the very worst) opens the organization up to a lawsuit. They either can't or don't want to tell you the real reason—and also, they are human . . . they don't want to hurt your feelings! Instead, try asking for advice. "How can I do better next time? Is there specific job experience that would be helpful?" Seeking advice for the future has more value than getting feedback on the past.

FIVE
Compensation Is More Than Money

The job offer you've been waiting for arrives! From the hundreds or even thousands of applicants, *you* are the one they want to hire. You've done such important work to earn this opportunity. Do a happy dance and woo-hoo out loud. But then take a pause.

I remember well the immense flood of relief and excitement I felt when I got my first job offer. Before the HR manager finished describing the position, and even before she started sharing the compensation package, I blurted out, "I accept!" Very kindly, the manager gave me some advice I have never forgotten and want to pass along to you. Express your enthusiasm and gratitude, but *do not* accept the offer on the spot. You've worked too hard to get here. Take a breath, say you'd like a day to consider, then do a bit more homework to identify what's on your must-have, would-like-to-have, and nice-but-not-a-dealbreaker list. It's time for frank discussions about compensation and negotiation.

Money Talk

Our attitudes about money show up in different ways. It has been widely reported that younger generations are more comfortable talking about sex than about personal finance. In fact, a whole new class of professionals

**The Hard Truth/
What Insiders Know**

There is always a little bit of flexibility, but you have to uncover how to unlock it.

is advertising their services as "financial therapists." Starting with how your family talked about money or avoided financial conversations, we can have barriers to discussing earnings or assumptions and beliefs about money—everyone does. And naturally, you would never walk up to somebody and say, "Hey, how much money do you make?" Let's explore how to get the answers to your questions about pay rates in a helpful way.

Do you define yourself primarily by measuring how much money you earn? Is someone who makes $150 an hour more important or valuable than someone earning $18 an hour? Often, people early in their careers can feel undervalued and under-compensated for their efforts, so it's helpful to put wages in the context of our capitalist, market-driven economy. It's not about what you think you should be paid. It's about the value your work generates for your employer.

Big picture, compensation is a reflection of specialization. If you are better at something than another person, they will pay you to do that thing for them or for the group. If we all lived on a farm, and I'm better at milking cows than I am at plowing fields, I'm creating more value for the farm in the barn than in the pasture. In any community, we think about specializing in jobs so that each of us is adding value according to our different skills and abilities, and this makes the group better off as a whole. In our society today, job specialization is highly valued. What does this have to do with your compensation? Well, we all need to figure out, "What am I really good at and how much will other people pay me to do that job well?"

Another nuance for people early on in their careers is understanding the difference between pay and compensation. We tend to invest too much significance in pay while overlooking the additional value possible within compensation.

I like to start by thinking about compensation in three buckets. The first bucket is the cash you earn through your wages plus the dollar value of a benefits package—the payroll money that goes into your bank account. The second bucket is the training or the skills you acquire that will help advance your career—this talent bucket represents compensation in your long-term career investment and value. The third bucket is how you feel about the work—your intrinsic happiness bucket. It is the gratification that only you can put a value on.

Strive to find the right balance for yourself among these three compensation buckets. Satisfaction and joy alone won't pay the bills. You have to figure out what the right amount for each bucket is for you. That balance may change over time as your life circumstances evolve. But at any given time, there is a market demand for your skills expressed as a dollar amount, and a minimum amount you need to pay your bills.

It's easiest to identify the amount of the first bucket because it is the actual dollars and cents that go into your account at the end of the pay period, plus the worth of various types of benefits.

Let's start by looking at this first bucket of compensation.

Compensation as Money Paid

To determine reasonable salary levels, use Google, Glassdoor, or even the company's own website to find out what comparable jobs pay. Factors like geographical location and cost of living can alter pay rates between metro New Jersey and rural West Virginia, for example, which will be reflected in the salary range. Recently, some states have passed legislation that requires companies to be transparent about their pay ranges for both hourly and salaried roles. It's worth knowing if these laws apply where you live.

When pay grades or levels are posted, typically the criteria are also shown. Someone without a college degree may enter at one level, while the next pay grade requires higher education. Generally, these are consistently applied and are not terribly flexible.

Also worth knowing are the different ways pay is allocated to different jobs in your company or your industry. Knowing the full range of possibilities helps you set more realistic expectations and make more informed choices. There might be a base salary. There might be a performance bonus. There might be short-term compensation, long-term compensation, matching retirement funds, or a commission structure. As a salesperson, you might have a "draw" on your commission. And then there are benefits that have a monetary value, things like medical and dental insurance or a 401k. The company might pay for education and training, enabling you to earn a certificate or a work-related advanced degree.

When I was looking to transition to a new company and a new industry, I knew nothing about all these differences. Fortunately, I reached out to someone who recently worked at the company I was interviewing for, and he graciously laid out all the facts for me. You're lucky to find someone like this person who explained so much to me. But even if you don't have that option, you should always ask the person making the offer to explain in fine detail, "How does compensation work?" That's a more comprehensive way of asking what the position offers, including but going beyond pay. What are the other valuable perks? Paid time off, sick leave, retirement savings, health and life insurance, education, training, family leave, pet insurance? It's potentially a long list that can mean real value for you and also offers some room for negotiation.

Even as this information becomes more transparent, it can still be vague and subject to interpretation. For example, in some states where organizations have to post the pay, they sometimes give a wide compensation range. It takes effort on your part to figure out the possibilities. Ask for advice from people knowledgeable about the industry, not just your family or friends. They may lead you to set too high or too low a figure by not asking for what is a reasonable, industry-standard compensation package.

Compensation as an Investment in Advancement

The second bucket is too often overlooked. Ask yourself how this position might set you up to advance in your career. There are times when the skills you will learn are so worthwhile that taking this job, for a lower amount than you thought was ideal, is actually a solid investment.

I've been listening to an FBI podcast that offers a great example. There's a special agent who, as a government employee, is in a very structured pay scale and overall pay program. It's impossible to earn more even though others at that same level are doing desk jobs and do not face the danger of his position. He could be the best special agent ever, but he's never going to exceed the salary of his pay grade. He wouldn't get crazy performance bonuses or stock in the organization or have the option to be promoted to FBI director . . . this isn't how their pay structure works.

But when I heard descriptions of the training he's receiving, I began to see his opportunities in another light. He has taken an investigator's course, trained on specialized photography for crime scenes, and earned an impressive list of certifications. These are all skills he did not have when he was hired, and now they can open new, more lucrative jobs for him. He is going to very interesting cases and seeing the most innovative investigative work in the world. So, although he is making the same salary as the guy in the desk job, he is gathering valuable skills that can help him learn, get promoted, start his own company, or move to a new field like private security with better earning power. He is earning career options—the kind that don't get deposited into a bank account.

Very often, employers offer tuition assistance or in-house specialized training. Doing any of this requires extra time and effort, but it is a low or no-cost way to add value to your resume. It is super important to know that you'll need to be a strong performer in your day job and a serious student at night to be worthy of the investment. Keep this in mind as you weigh the salary you are being offered against your time commitment and the value of having the company invest in your professional development.

Compensation as Personal Fulfillment

The third bucket is, without a doubt, the most personal and

unique. Sometimes we only discover what we value most about a job when we've made a poor decision. We believe that because we like helping people, we should become a doctor or nurse only to find out we faint at the sight of blood, or worse, sometimes sick people aren't nice to the people who take care of them! OK, that's extreme, but what we imagine a job will be like is often not the reality. You may be making a lot of money but feel unfulfilled by the work. Or you may want to save the world, and find your job is not doing enough to bring about immediate, positive results.

How much do you want to love what you do? Do you dread Mondays and live for Friday afternoons? Are you putting in time before you can live your life? Don't get me wrong. All work, no matter how exciting or highly paid, has its moments of boredom, frustration, setbacks, and even total failures. It's not a matter of work being easy, thrilling, and full of rewards every day.

All work has its downsides but get in touch with what makes you happy in a job. Take, for example, a park ranger whose job is to patrol Yosemite National Park to protect endangered species. Many people would look at that job and say, "You could not pay me enough to do that. It's lonely, dangerous, too hot or too cold, and unbelievably boring." But the right person for the job says, "I can't believe I get paid to do this. It's awesome."

Maybe you want to tackle some social issues that you believe need attention, like hunger, homelessness, or rural poverty. The fact is, nonprofit work often pays less than a comparable position in a for-profit firm. You might find your reward in making a difference in the lives of people in your community. Another source of satisfaction is being energized and inspired by the people you work with. Does your work support the values you hold most important? Remember that FBI agent? He went to work joyous that he was able to serve his community and make the world safer every day. The third bucket of compensation is about how well your job meets your needs for meaning and personal gratification.

The Fine Art of Negotiation

You are getting an offer. Congratulations. First, say thank you and reiterate that you are excited about the job. Then, it is time to get started on getting to an agreement that works for you and the company.

The best way to start a negotiation is to gather all the facts. Too often, applicants rush to the base salary or the bonus potential, but it is helpful to spend time at the beginning of a conversation with the hiring manager or HR representative to review all the components of compensation. Please don't interrupt them when they deliver the offer details. Take careful notes.

Honesty helps. If this is your first salaried job, lead with the truth. "Miss Smith, this is my first corporate offer, and I have a lot of questions. Can you take some extra time to walk me through all the details?" It is also helpful to understand what role this person has in following up. Is she the person you should contact for clarifications and requests, or will that be someone else?

Don't enter this negotiation like a hostile takeover. Listen carefully and ask questions in a thoughtful, polite way. You don't want to negotiate too hard and be seen as greedy and unreasonable, but you do want to advocate for what best meets your needs. It is a delicate balance.

After you understand the parts of the offer, it's fine to ask about the options for advancement. This can also signal that you are interested in a long-term relationship with the company. If you're quoted an hourly wage, you should understand what training is available and how it might be possible to earn more. Ask about benefits and when you are eligible for them. Make sure you are touching on every aspect of compensation that matters to you. Listen for when the response is "no" or "maybe" to see where there may be room to negotiate.

Assuming you still really want this job, be a partner in the hiring process by being realistic. The compensation has to be in the zip code for what you need and can reasonably expect.

It's not solely about what you want, need, or think you should have. It's what the current market for your skills, with your experience, in this industry, in your town, is willing to pay. Be clear about what matters most to you, what is acceptable, and what is a deal breaker. If you say at the start, "I'm really flexible," you're signaling anything goes.

On the other hand, don't hold out for the impossible. If you're making $20 an hour, you should not be negotiating for a $350 an hour job. You might think you can handle a management role that pays $200k a year, but realistically, how much you make *today* is a reflection of the value you create for your current company. It's possible to double or triple your pay in your next role, but there has to be a compelling reason why you're not earning that salary now.

So how do you know if you should accept their "best offer?" It is always worth asking, "Is that the best you can do?" and listening for the response. Don't take the job if it is not going to be enough to meet your needs. Don't count on vague promises about automatic promotions or raises. The folks making promises about future promotions often mean the best, but you can't guarantee they will be at the company when that automatic raise was supposed to happen. Ask to get all promises in writing. If they can't put it in writing, acknowledge to yourself this is a risk, and ask yourself if this is a risk worth taking—sometimes it is.

Even as you advance in your career, negotiation remains a part of the hiring process. When one acquaintance posed the "Is that your best offer?" question, the employer bumped the base pay by $20,000! A friend was asked to apply for a job with an organization in need of her specific skill set. When they made an offer, it was for a junior

**Helpful Hack/
What Insiders Do**

Don't take the first offer. Say thank you, sleep on it, and do your homework.

Phone a friend to get an unemotional, informed opinion.

Help them hire you by having informed, reasonable, and clear expectations.

leadership role, far below her level of expertise. Instead of walking away in disgust, she made clear that there was some miscommunication, and she was interested in an executive-level role . . . and executive compensation. If they couldn't offer that, she suggested they hire her as a consultant at her market rate. Being able to reposition the role and its compensation turned into a win-win for both parties.

Bottom line, you have to be comfortable with the offer you get on day one. The hiring manager's job is to hire you for the least amount possible, but an amount that will get you to stay for a really long time. It's up to you to know if the opportunity fully compensates you in money, professional development, and personal satisfaction.

PART TWO
Getting Ahead

With smart effort, diligence, luck, and determination (plus your personal awesomeness), you've landed what you believe will be a great job with a great company. If you don't want to find yourself doing the same stuff at the same desk for the next five years, Part Two is for you.

In Part One, while you were trying to find work, it was all about you listening to yourself. What are your goals? What are your hopes and dreams? Now, when we're talking about getting ahead, your orientation is all about the rest of the world. Because if you want to accomplish your goals, you have to work within an ecosystem, and to do that, you have to work with and observe other people. You have to listen to the market. If you want to be a leader, you have to develop an orientation toward what other people need. If you're in sales, product development, research, or a teammate on some internal project, you have to listen to your customer(s).

Part Two offers specific advice on some of the skills you should acquire to help you gain traction and move ahead in your career journey. Success isn't accidental. We'll explore the positive impact of listening (chapter six), storytelling (chapter seven), and routine (chapter eight), practices often assumed but more often missing from our professional skill sets.

Kaboom

Before we go there, I want to introduce one of my favorite

pieces of advice for early-stage professionals. If you want to distinguish yourself in your company, no matter what level you're currently at, find a *Shit Bomb* and run toward it.

What is a Shit Bomb? It's the thing that is making life miserable for everybody. It's toxic, and no one wants to touch it. It's impossible to solve. It's "the way we've always done it." It's the f-ed up situation everybody blames on somebody else (usually someone higher in the org chart). "I can't believe we have to (fill in the blank). It's a huge waste of time. It's totally screwing up my project/department/customers, but my manager/VP/CEO is too lazy/clueless/afraid to fix it."

It could also be something terrible that is going on in your town or the world. Does your community have a tragic homelessness crisis? Is your local river polluted? Is there a promising local politician who has no chance of winning a state-wide election? Jump on it.

Run toward that problem. It's a problem that requires your attention. If you fix it, you're a star.

Everybody knows your name. They know you aren't afraid to take on the tough stuff. They see you're able to make something happen that is better for everyone. They see you add real value. You've done more than solve a problem. You've set yourself up to be a go-to person for the hard challenges that move a career.

I knew a young scientist in his post-grad years struggling to find a problem he could take on. He encountered an old, grizzly, leathery-skinned scientist whose milky eyes were the result of decades of intense sun exposure while conducting research in the Antarctic. He told the post-grad, "You need to find something really hard where you can learn about yourself and try to make the world a better place. Find something you're passionate about, put in the time to learn, and be a doer." The post-doc went to Asia, where he founded an environmental nonprofit. He spent 10 years learning, marshaling resources, and building community. It taught him more than environmental science. He learned how to get people on board with a project, and it put him in touch with the real environmental impact on real people's lives. Only later did he realize he'd found his Shit Bomb.

Now in his 60s, he is a world-renowned leader. He helped form an entire United Nations effort. He encourages younger people with his charismatic vision of building their expertise while getting worthwhile things done.

There's another approach to learning from the Shit Bomb, and that's taking on a losing cause. I met a woman recently who worked in politics. Early on in her career, someone gave her the odd advice to work for a candidate who was likely to lose. As you can imagine, not many people were volunteering to work for a "loser." But it meant that she had responsibility far beyond her experience. She opened the campaign office with a card table and a phone. Period. She was head of fundraising, advance logistics, and communications. She was the head of . . . everything. During an early debate, her candidate nailed a few questions with some impressive statements that made social media explode. Suddenly, he was the "it" person in the campaign spotlight. Just as suddenly, she was now running a national fundraising effort. The momentum didn't last, and her guy eventually dropped out of the race, but she looks back on this time as the most intense learning experience imaginable. She learned so much about herself—Where am I great? Where do I struggle? Who should I hire? How do I craft a powerful message? When there's more to do than is humanly possible, how do I prioritize? She took this hard job when she was young and able to keep crazy hours and sleep on couches. But what she learned by running at this Shit Bomb opened amazing career opportunities to her at an early age.

Day one in your new job is not too soon to start searching for the Shit Bomb you will run toward. Acquiring the skills we'll cover in Part Two will help you be the bomb defusing hero.

SIX
Deep Listening

In the bad old times of parenting, there was a popular expression that "children should be seen and not heard." If you've spent any time around children, you know they do not agree. Even before they can talk, babies want us to hear them. The truth is, we all want to be heard. Listening leads to learning and learning leads to understanding. So in this way, actively listening to another person is incredibly powerful.

Genuine listening doesn't mean simply not talking. And it doesn't mean mentally composing your reply so you're ready to fire away when the other person stops speaking. In every single business (or for that matter, human) interaction, you have to listen. You have to be curious and work at decoding what is being said. Listening equals learning! What do people care about? How are they making a decision? What motivates them? Even in negotiation for your own compensation or negotiating a price on a product or a service, listening is key. You have to understand the buyer and the buying process. You have to listen to understand a customer, a person you supervise or mentor, your boss, and your coworkers. Uber has an algorithm that "listens" to demand and responds by switching to surge pricing. In a human situation, you won't have 1000 people requesting a ride; you have to listen hard to do your own

**The Hard Truth/
What Insiders Know**

If you really pay attention, people will tell you who they are.

People will tell you what they want.

adjusting of priorities and process.

Find out what motivates your boss and what his/her goals are. What happens when your boss achieves their goals? On what factors are you going to be evaluated at the end of the year? This process of understanding performance expectations and consequences happens at every level of an organization, including what the board expects from the CEO. Pay attention to what's going on all around you. Why do certain people seem to be more successful? What can you learn from listening to and working with them?

Make Listening Fun

OK, you think you're already a great listener, so let's see how well you do. Practice pair and share in a low-risk environment. Get a friend, family member, or your favorite barista to tell you something interesting they did recently. Listen intently. Repeat it back to them, with extra points if you can use some of the same language the speaker used (that's really empathetic and an advanced listening skill). You're not after a word-for-word repetition. You're trying to show that you totally heard and understood everything they told you. Do it at a party. Have someone tell you about themselves and then introduce them to someone else. It never fails that if you've really heard the person and manage to share who they are with another person, they will think you're amazing and like you for it.

At work, when your boss gives you an assignment, repeat it back to show you've got it. Asking "Did I get this right?" builds rapport and helps you avoid doing unnecessary, irrelevant or useless work. At the end of a meeting, don't leave without being really clear about any assignments. "This is what I heard were next steps. What's the timeline? Friday? Or is next week soon enough?"

If you want to learn from a pro, go on a sales call with an experienced leader. Watch what they do, how they do it, and listen to what they say. Chances are, they will do less talking than listening. You'll see them be curious and ask questions of their customers: What are your problems? What is changing in your business? What keeps you up at night? How has your current (product/service) been working for you? How do they handle any uncomfortable information they might get back about their products or services?

The Ones Worth Listening To

When you're the newbie, everyone deserves your attention, no matter what role they hold in the organization. You can learn a lot by speaking to people with different perspectives, for example, the line worker versus the vice president. Take the time to understand their perspective, and their role and influence within the company. It may not be apparent from their title. Pay attention to what they say and do and how it affects you. Don't "write somebody off" without paying attention to their needs. Dismissing people with a "You're not the boss of me" attitude can backfire and badly damage your reputation. One of my mentees found herself in a situation where she outranks someone who is not her formal supervisor but has a lot of power. She thought she could ignore his directives because, in her mind, she thought, "I don't have to answer to you." She has unfortunately found out that she should have paid more attention, regardless of the org chart, because this person has tremendous informal power. Not someone you want to get on the wrong side of, ever.

Over time, you will learn to distinguish between people who just want to talk and people who have something thoughtful or valuable to say. Find people you feel comfortable with, but don't make the mistake of only hanging out with people who are exactly like you.

In my career, I've found it helpful to have a battle buddy, someone going through some of the same things, so I could check in and say, "Does this sound right to you?" Search out someone who agrees with or at least is sympathetic to you, but always get additional information from someone you trust who can be objective. It's often very valuable to get advice from your parents! And it's a proven strong move to find a mentor (formal or informal) in your workplace. It's probably not possible to follow every bit of advice you get, but as they say in AA meetings, take what you like and leave the rest. Just be grateful for anyone who is willing to help you.

Why Listening Matters

A friend came to me recently after he'd been laid off and was struggling to find a new job. At first, everything I suggested he rejected. So I realized I was making a bunch of assumptions about him, and I needed to get more information. Like most of us, I often come into these conversations with an assumption that the person's life is this way or that way, or they're making this decision because they are financially motivated, or they are not a big risk-taker, or whatever. But a lot of times, I'm not really right. I've had to listen to discover that I've made assumptions that are totally wrong. A big part of implicit bias is where you think people are making decisions because they are like you. And that's not true. People make all kinds of decisions for all kinds of different reasons.

With my friend, I needed to stop talking and start listening. The next conversation started with the "6 Whys," the idea that you keep going deeper by asking a series of questions that help uncover the real issue: "Why don't you want to do X? Why do you think that feels like 'selling out'? Why are you reluctant to apply for this position?" and more.

Listening to his answers showed me how badly eroded his confidence was. If I was going to help him move forward, it wasn't going to be by suggesting jobs he should apply for. We had to work on restoring his belief in his abilities and confidence in his market value. And he has to make a decision that finding a job is more important than nursing his wounded pride or fearing rejection. If I hadn't switched to asking questions and listening for the truth, then mirroring it back to him, we would never have found the real problems holding him back and keeping him miserable and unemployed.

Developing effective listening skills delivers so many rewards. Good listeners:

- Make fewer mistakes
- Waste less time being confused
- Avoid disappointing their boss/customer/partner
- Experience lower levels of frustration

**Helpful Hack/
What Insiders Do**

Speak less, listen more.

Ask clarifying questions.

Check their assumptions at the door.

They also gain the respect and cooperation of other employees or the loyalty of good customers. Being really listened to makes us all feel seen and valued. It helps build stronger relationships of trust and confidence, and shows you to be reliable and honest. Do these sound like traits that can affect your advancement in the company? Well, no guarantee, but for sure, being a good listener will never hold you back.

SEVEN
Beyond Bedtime:
Storytelling in Business and Life

Have you heard the one about the kid with a mark on his forehead and unusual powers? Or the one about the scruffy band of rebels intent on saving the galaxy? Or maybe about a group of mismatched twenty-somethings who seem to spend most of their time in and out of each other's apartments? Then there's the ultra-wealthy hanging out in posh vacation locations around the globe. Whether it's *Harry Potter, Star Wars, Friends*, or *The White Lotus*, stories capture our attention.

Since the caveman days, human beings have uniquely used stories to inform, instruct, and inspire. Consider just how long great stories endure. The Bible, Shakespeare, Charles Dickens, *The Catcher in the Rye, Jaws, The Lord of the Rings*, and even (or especially) the tale of the doomed Titanic. These have been told over many years and still have the power to move us. So what does this have to do with business and leadership? Everything.

Leading Is a Journey

In business, storytelling is a way of creating a picture in people's minds of what you want to accomplish. It is a powerful way of expressing your vision as a leader. Storytelling advances the career of leaders because it helps people get on board with what they

The Hard Truth/ What Insiders Know

Stories have more power than facts.

want to achieve. When people identify emotionally with the picture you present, the impact is much greater than any you can affect through data, lists of facts, charts, or graphs. Good stories mean more to us than anything else.

The very process of creating a story can also help you work out a specific image so that you know what your goals are. It's the difference between saying, "I will work hard," and telling yourself, "I want to work hard so I can buy a car for cash." You don't have to specify the amount of money in the bank. The signal is clear to your brain: you want to be secure enough that you don't have to take out a car loan. At work, your goal might sound something like, "I want the client to be so happy that they recommend us to everyone they know."

Even when it's difficult for you to describe the specifics of your goals for yourself or your company, you want to do your best to create a picture of what the optimal result looks like. When you describe the outcome, that picture stays in people's minds, even without detailing every step along the way. In fact, the lack of detail in your story can provide motivation for your co-workers or your partners. By providing a vision of the end result, but not the path to get there, you're giving your team (and yourself) freedom to innovate, experiment, and do something remarkable. Let's say your goal is to grow sales in your department to a level that enables the company to launch a new product or service. The end goal opens up all those possibilities for everyone to take some ownership of getting to success. That's one of the reasons why succesful CEOs routinely use storytelling to drive growth as well as innovation.

Leaders need to lead in a clear direction and convince followers to not just go along but to actively be part of building success. Storytelling is a tool that inspires, and inspiration is the force behind commitment. Effective leaders help people take ownership of how each individual in the enterprise is able to contribute to and benefit from reaching a shared vision.

Make It Memorable

Some years ago, I was interviewing candidates for a highly desirable role as a CEO in an incredible mission-oriented organization with a lot of complexity. We began to think that former hospital CEOs would be great fits for this unique role. Naturally, one of the routine questions we asked was why the candidate wanted this particular position. One applicant paused a moment, sat back in the chair, and told me this story:

"I was 17 years old, working as an orderly at a hospital where my mother worked as a nurse. One day, a fire broke out in one of the hospital rooms. Without thinking about it or being asked to help, I grabbed an emergency fire hose in the hallway and ran toward the blaze. I was a strong football player, running really hard, pulling that hose as it unspooled behind me. Suddenly, still yards away from the burning room, I was flat on my back in the corridor. I had run out of hose, and the impact from yanking that short hose completely flipped me over. What I remember most about that day was how mad I felt about that crappy hose. We got the fire out, but that wasn't the end of it for me. I marched right down to the hospital CEO's office and told him how upset I was that this stupid hose was worthless. Why didn't we have better equipment? Remarkably, that CEO listened to my teenage rant and for two hours we talked about how important hospital administration is. When I left his office, a 17-year-old football-playing high school kid, I knew that I was going to be the CEO of a hospital someday. For 20 years, I have been at progressively bigger and more complex hospitals, making lives better for patients and caregivers."

Boom. Mic drop.

Here's the funny thing. Years later, I remember all the details of this story but nothing else, not where the job was or who the guy was. It was his story that made the lasting impression.

What makes a story memorable? Think about the stories you love. There's a conflict of some kind, some problem clearly identified, then the added sizzle of details that make the situation real. The adjectives that you use are the spice. When you put the ingredients together, you're not just delivering a plain baked potato. It's loaded with chives and pepper, creamy salted butter, and grated cheese. It's hot and gooey with a crispy skin right from the oven, and you're the chef. Make it exciting, immediate, and visual, but keep it real. No one wants to hear about that fish that keeps getting bigger with each telling. Hyperbole is like overdoing the spice. No one will swallow it.

As you work on identifying your stories, find ways to test out your bits. Tell stories at the dinner table, try out tales during drinks with your friends. Look for the things that work, the parts of the story that resonated with your listeners. There are tons of examples of legendary storytellers among all kinds of politicians: Winston Churchill, Martin Luther King Jr.'s "I Have a Dream" speech, Reagan's "Mr. Gorbachev, bring down that wall." Religious leaders, filmmakers, rappers, bloggers, TikTokers, and writers are all spinning stories. Break it down to understand what the story arc is: the setup, the conflict, the ending, and the lessons learned.

Build your true story based on conflicts, inner drama, or the moral dilemma of a fight against yourself. Situations like these unlock a connection with other human beings. Adjectives draw us in as listeners. We want to place ourselves in the scene. We see ourselves in your story as part of our common experience.

Then, most importantly, know when to stop talking.

Know Your Audience

If you have some level of emotional intelligence, you understand that various situations call for different behaviors. What's okay at Mardi Gras isn't the right look for your quarterly team meeting. The gossip you pick up at the watercooler (another form of storytelling by the way) most likely isn't what should be repeated to your supervisor.

Stand-up comics excel at reading their audience and tailoring their jokes to fit the room. Similarly, you have to be attentive to what the right story is for the listener you're addressing. Am I talking to my husband or wife? Am I talking to my fellow teammates on this project? Am I the leader or a peer? Am I pitching my company's C-suite execs on a new product or service? The core of the story may be consistent, but how I tell the story might be a little bit different depending on who is in the room. Or maybe I need to pivot to another story entirely.

An executive who was a highly skilled storyteller once shared with me his belief that "everybody has four stories: one personal success, one personal failure, one professional success, and one professional failure. With those stories, you can pretty much answer anything or inspire somebody." That strikes me as a pretty great insight. Having a short list of stories certainly saved me when I misjudged my audience during a crucial job interview.

When I was transitioning from the military to a corporate job, I wanted to share what by that point had been one of the biggest leadership challenges of my life. We'd been working a grueling schedule of 24/7 operations, securing airfields and critical locations across South Korea since September 11. During this time, my unit had performed exceptionally well, working nearly six months nonstop. As company commander, I joined my exhausted team in the field for dinner—we hadn't eaten in the mess hall for months because we simply didn't have time. Out of respect for my team and to show solidarity with them, officers always eat last, so I was at the end of the chow line. By the time I reached the buffet line, all that was left was a pan of limp green beans. So that's what I had for dinner. I thought by telling this story I was sharing the extent of our unit's operations and how selfless I was capable of being. But I could see the interviewer didn't care and didn't get it. "Oh crap," I thought, "I've lost her." So before she could end the interview, I quickly switched to another short story.

I described how, when I had been the supply officer for my unit, I'd negotiated for these awesome Cannondale bikes. I was able to get them at a great price for the military police unit, and the bikes represented a major, cool equipment upgrade that the soldiers loved. That story lit her interest. To me, this was nothing special, actually kind of a dumb story, but it's the one she could relate to. Who is in your audience really matters.

The guy who told me about everyone having four stories had a 9/11 story of his own. In the aftermath of the attack, he was supposed to be leading his daughter's Girl Scout troop on a campout. After the world witnessed this horrific tragedy, everything seemed scary and dangerous. He told the story of meeting with the other troop leader dads to figure out what they should do. They knew how much their daughters had been looking forward to doing arts and crafts together, making s'mores around a campfire, and being with their dads. The men decided that what their daughters needed most was to be with family and friends in a safe, fun environment. The dads went ahead with the campout.

This executive later told his story in answer to the final question of his CEO interview. It was a way of demonstrating that he understood that real leadership is showing up for those who need you in the way they need you, not necessarily the way you had in mind or feel comfortable doing. Leaders need to prove that they will consistently be there for their teams, no matter what. By the way, he got that job.

Less is Always More

Your goal should be to tell a story that is memorable, that locks into your listener's deep attention. It entertains, it engages them, but there's something extra powerful about getting them to picture themselves in that small drama. Too much information is too hard to follow. Aim to create a sharp, clear image that the listener can follow and even recall.

How do you give them this image? It is not through spinning a very long, twisty story that goes back and forth for 10 endless minutes. That story gets lost. Even if you keep your listener attentive to the end, that story will not last in their mind. A story has to be long enough to hold space for some drama, maybe even some pain. It takes work to be brief. It takes more work to deliver your short message without mumbling or stumbling. That's why I say prepare, practice, and polish, but don't lose the immediacy and emotional power. Deliver your story with so much power that it could have happened yesterday.

It's Always Story Hour Somewhere

There's no shortage of occasions or opportunities for storytelling in a corporate environment. When you think about it, we are each telling a story at work every single day. And we are consciously or subconsciously reacting to the stories other people are telling us.

Many times, the story telegraphs more than your or a leader's vision—it implies their values. Someone recently told me that he aspired to work for a big Wall Street firm until he saw the CEO walking down Fifth Avenue with a pretty young girl on each arm. He told me that this wasn't the image or example he wanted in a leader. His story—and this image—was powerful to him. In that image, he saw a man and, by extension, a company with different values than his. That story changed his career trajectory. Working for a values-aligned company meant more to him than chasing a position in a prestige brand. His story also told me about his values and deepened my respect for him. I could see him on the street, and in my mind's eye, I pictured his boss. Simple. Memorable.

Stories can be nearly as valuable as bonuses and awards. Use them when you conduct your weekly team meeting. Tell the story of a peer doing great work, an example of Sara being so fantastic for the input and impact she makes on our team. Tell stories about hope or change or the seasons and cycles of your business. These are opportunities for you to create the values of your company—and share your personal values.

Classic storytelling moments often occur during corporate retreats, annual meetings, and moments of crisis. Do you remember how early in the COVID-19 pandemic everyone was almost in a constant state of panic? Some people were afraid, and rightly so, that even if they stayed healthy, they could lose their job and whole livelihood. Early on, a leader I know had one of those all-hands Zooms. Employees were skeptical, but they joined. He was a straight-talker, and he didn't mince words, letting everyone know that "many of us in this virtual room" have been through hard times and a great deal of uncertainty. He shared specifically how the global financial crisis in 2008-09 wrecked the business. He said, "We came back then, and we will now. Our backs are against the wall, and now is the moment to

> **Helpful Hack/ What Insiders Do**
>
> One good story is all you need. Don't over-do it. Keep it punchy, vivid, and above all, short.

call your clients, to be proactive, to fight." He gave his team confidence by reminding some of them of their own success story and by giving others a picture of safety. Then, he even gave a roadmap to follow. You could see heads nodding – not just the new joiners and younger people – but the veterans too. This did more to lift spirits and give hope than any fancy PowerPoint could do.

Recently, I heard a CEO share a story about going to a classical music concert. The performance featured a pianist who apparently was not happy with her rendition. After concluding the first piece, she rose from her bench and began to walk off stage. The conductor quietly caught up with her and had a private word. The audience had no way of knowing what was said, but the pianist returned to her seat and finished the performance with renewed energy and passion. Later, he asked the conductor what he said. The conductor had whispered, "We do it because we love the music."

The CEO uses this story to illustrate a number of points we can all recognize: Things don't always go as planned. We sometimes disappoint ourselves. Frustration can be part of every effort. But a leader has to be there for us, motivating each player and keeping the ensemble and the soloists moving forward even in the midst of setbacks. He's trying to give an image that sparks something great in his audience. He's telling us that fostering grit, persistence, and resilience is not just his job. It's something we can all do for others too.

EIGHT
Consistency Is a Superpower

In 2014, four-star admiral and former Navy SEAL William McRaven delivered a motivational commencement address at the University of Texas at Austin. Since then, over 40 million viewers have watched his speech on YouTube. This accomplished man, who, among other things, led the operation that resulted in the death of the 9/11 terrorist, Osama Bin Laden, gave a talk that offered key practices for changing the world. His first bit of advice? Make your bed every morning.

McRaven knows from decades of military discipline and leadership excellence that having a solid routine is the foundation for achievement. Making your bed seems dumb. How could this basic act do anything for me as a person or as a professional? What difference could it possibly make in my day, my week, my life?

I encourage you to watch the entire video clip, but here's the first insight. Making your bed starts your day with a task done well. It prepares you to face the day with a sense of accomplishment and competence. That's like putting on a suit of armor. You are ready for whatever lies ahead. And let's be honest. Every day is full of surprises, good, bad, or neutral, whether they happen at home or at work. Having a routine that puts you in control, if

**The Hard Truth/
What Insiders Know**

Human beings easily become slaves to their habits. If you don't choose and manage your habits, they control you.

only for the early morning hours, gives you a real advantage.

Know Your Habits

Before you can create positive routines, you have to recognize what habits you consciously or unconsciously already have. We all have them, and often without our knowing it, they run our lives.

Think about the structure of your week. What are the things you do every day? These should include work and leisure activities, with perhaps special attention to how you start and end your days. Are you skipping breakfast so you can sleep a bit later? Are you stressing about traffic as you try to get to work on time? Are you constantly trying to do one more thing at work that causes you to show up late for meetings? Does your day end with you feeling exhausted on the sofa, eating ice cream, and hitting "Next episode" on Netflix? I'm not here to judge. You be the judge. Which of your routines serve you and which are holding you back from feeling productive, positive, and energized? Only you can answer that.

Once you've done your honest assessment of what's working for or against you, pick just one habit you want to change. What if you went to bed 30 minutes earlier so you could wake up in time for coffee and breakfast to start your day? What if you scheduled your gym visits in the morning instead of after work, when you're often too tired to go? What if instead of just texting your friend, you met up on the weekend for drinks or a walk? What if you did make your bed every morning? Breaking an old habit and building a new one takes discipline, time, and self-kindness. Expect some setbacks and even some failures. But being able to persist is a habit, too, and a powerful one.

How Habits Help

I've learned through hundreds of interviews with executives, managers, and everyday observations of people I admire that having a purposeful routine has helped them be successful.

People talk about how their routine can be calming in difficult times and how it allows them to exert some control over chaos. There's no such thing as smooth sailing despite our best planning efforts. But professional and personal success is less about what happens to you and more about how you handle all the ups and downs. Successful leaders attribute having a routine and good habits to helping them navigate the stormy seas.

I'm calling out corporate leaders, but I've found most successful and happy people have personal routines too. I saw this when I was in high school and had the opportunity to get to know a bit about the home life of my Home Ec teacher. She was someone I greatly admired. She was a wonderful, caring teacher and advisor to the student council. Once, when I had to drop something off at her house on a Saturday, she told me, "You're welcome to stop by but not until 1 PM." What I found out was that every Saturday, she and her kids had a "game" of chores, with each one responsible for certain tasks to keep the household running smoothly. Every Saturday morning was the same, no matter what. Then there'd be a simple lunch, and by 1 PM, order restored and chores complete, it was time to enjoy the weekend. Creating this routine for herself and her family was a stress reliever for her, taught her kids responsibility but also the pleasure of shared accomplishment. Happier at home means happier at school and work!

All organizations operate within a set of routines. Recognizing what your company's routines are helps provide predictability. This is especially true for work teams. Whether it takes the form of daily check-ins, weekly meetings, or a calendar of milestones, routines allow team members to budget their time, prepare for planned events, and know how the required work is progressing (or not). Having an awareness that some specific thing happens every Tuesday at 10 AM or every third Thursday helps you and everyone around you know what is expected.

When a generally shared and accepted routine is in place, it creates a system that helps people thrive inside the organization.

In my company, for example, we have a detailed process for a new client launch. We start out with a timeline and map out all the markers we need to hit: stakeholder engagement briefings, internal launch, then the client launch meeting, etc. That process provides my team with a clear roadmap and helps us handle whatever variables or unexpected developments that might arise with a particular client or particular situation. After each client engagement, my team reviews our process to see where it might be improved. We want to add in things that made us successful and take out anything that fell short.

If you're an athlete participating in any sport at any level, you already know about evaluating your routine. Elite athletes are looking for ways to shave milliseconds off their times, or ways to protect themselves from injury. Even casual sport enthusiasts think about the way they warm up and cool down, about the intensity of their workouts and the performance enhancing quality of their gear. Habits should never detract from our ability to perform. A habit's role is not to create stress; it's to remove it.

Build Your Routine

Management professionals and consultants often talk about creating frameworks as a way to improve a company's performance. Framework is another way of describing a methodology, a planning process, an annual schedule, or an operational plan. Every sport, school, industry, and business has a way they think about and structure operating day to day. In education, it's the school year broken into semesters with summers off. In business or government, it's a fiscal year that may or may not align with the calendar year.

Frameworks are like routines. They help organize many aspects of an enterprise into a calendar, a set of expected events, and important milestones. All of us have experienced the power of a framework during the academic schedule. Families made important decisions about vacations, changing jobs, and moving, shaped by the school year. In the business fiscal year, budgeting processes and audits are big drivers of how an organization operates.

There are macro routines that define your company, but there are also numerous micro routines as part of the framework of your organization. Does your CEO offer informal chats over regularly scheduled coffee breaks? Does your team go out for a group lunch on Fridays? Does your supervisor hold a meeting to review what just happened in an earlier meeting? Routine behaviors might also be informal expectations like attending a golf outing, taking part in an awards event, serving on the company holiday committee or going out for drinks with the team (especially hard if you're not a drinker). It might be bigger habits like flying all over the country to attend conferences. Don't feel bad if you can't do it all. But make the extra effort to show up for the ones that really count. Respect the company's expected behavior, but figure out at this point in your career how these routines and expectations can serve you. Be on the lookout for habits that help, be wary of habits that don't, and be mindful of how important each of these is to the company.

For your own habit building, think about what routines empower you in your specific situation today that make you better. I have routines in my fitness practice that I find useful in my work life. As a runner, I divide my workouts into sprint days and distance days. At work, that translates into sprint days when I am making 25 to 50 client calls and powering through the day. As a friend says, I'm in the red zone on the work meter. On other days, I'm doing longer projects solo or with my team that require more critical thinking, research, decision making, and collaboration. These work styles require very different skills as if they're two very different muscles.

In my personal life, every morning I have coffee with my husband, and I hold that time as sacred and wonderful. It starts my day off right. I make my bed (thank you, General McRaven), and then we have family time at night. Bracketing my workday with my domestic routine has helped me handle times when things go bad, and life doesn't go the way I planned. The dog barfs in my running shoes. It rains on the parade. Whatever. I know I have my comforting and reassuring routines to fall back on.

I hope you're convinced that forming positive habits is worth the effort, but I have to warn you that habits can also have a downside. When a habit becomes an addiction, trouble is brewing. If you become so attached to your routine that nothing can disrupt or displace it, even in unusual circumstances, you've fallen into the trap of inflexibility. It happens to people who are unwilling to change or adapt by modifying a habit, and it happens at an organizational level too. In business, the red flag warning is hearing "that's the way we've always done it," a sure sign of rigidity and refusal to innovate. Is there a process or practice your team is stuck with that only causes friction, leads to mistakes, or wastes effort? Are you perpetuating that habit because change is uncomfortable, and it's easier to keep doing what you've always done? Insiders know that examining old habits is essential. Inviting a fresh perspective, challenging old assumptions, and asking if this routine is still serving us is the way companies continue to thrive. The same process applies to us as individuals. While I'm no fan of New Year's resolutions, the start of a new year, a birthday, or an anniversary offers fruitful times for reflecting on our routines to see if the time is right for a change.

Spillover Effect

Thoughtfully and realistically building your own personal and professional routine helps you to handle stress, work at your best, bring calmness and order to chaos, and gives you some brain time to think about the things that are really important instead of dithering over every little thing. You might think of having a routine like having a school uniform. Putting it on every day saves precious mind space for more pressing decisions.

Organizations use routine to create the discipline that results in the basics done consistently and well. Having a solid operational routine makes it possible to shoot for greater aspirational goals that move the company forward and give it a competitive advantage. As a team leader or good team member, having a proven methodology gets you into the flow of greater productivity. You've seen it in action during a sales presentation when the team is so in sync, they're able to finish each other's sentences. They understand the processes and procedures built over time that define the way they operate.

**Helpful Hack/
What Insiders Do**

They create habits that are positive and confidence-building.

Their habits remove the need to make less important decisions (like what to wear to work) while avoiding becoming super rigid (it doesn't mean a navy suit and white shirt every day).

In daily life, having a routine that fills us with confidence and energy allows us to participate more fully in our professional and personal lives. We are more likely to reach out to other people and find time to engage with them. The result can be making rewarding personal and professional contacts, expanding our network, finding new friendships, and building community relationships that enrich and enhance every aspect of a fulfilling life.

PART THREE
Getting a Good Life

This morning, I'm writing in a favorite coffeeshop, a café where the barista knows my order before I key it into the kiosk. Above the ordering station, there's one of those motto wooden signs. This one says, "The happiest people don't have the best of everything. They just make the best of everything." You can groan or do an eye roll. But to me, this is a solid truth, with actual science to back up the claim.

By the time you've read your way through to this page, I very much hope you've found insights and practices that help you get a good job and find ways to thrive in it. You might recall that Part One was largely about listening to yourself first as you try to find the right career. Part Two offered specific advice on active listening, storytelling, and establishing a routine, skills to help you gain traction and move ahead in your journey by building leadership skills that turn that job into a career. You are starting to focus on other people. My experiences as a soldier, a business professional, a wife and mother, a swimmer and triathlete, and as an individual all point to one conclusion: A fulfilling life has to make space for you to hold and enjoy multiple roles, space and time to be able to care for yourself and for others at home, at work, and in your larger community.

Part Three offers advice and examples for building a life large enough for you, those you love, and those you lead. Whether at home, at work, or as a volunteer, effective leadership starts with authentically engaging your whole self with the many other people you will encounter. It's about positively shaping your response to the unexpected, the inevitable setbacks, the frustrations, and the outright failures. It's about finding ways to form meaningful, sustainable connections with friends, family, coworkers, neighbors, and even, at times, total strangers. Gratitude. Openness. That's what Part Three encourages you to practice. There is no downside to investing your time and effort while getting better at these ways of moving through the world.

NINE
An Attitude of Gratitude

One of the colleagues I most admire has a phrase he's known for, "You have to step back to lead forward." He doesn't mean rehashing everything that came before, the good and the bad. He doesn't mean dodging a bullet or letting someone else fill the void. He's encouraging leaders to pause, to take time to reflect, to pull back enough to get a wider view, to be able to consider multiple points of view. In short, to get outside of ourselves before we react or take action.

Pausing is a simple act but one that is increasingly hard to let ourselves do. We are all constantly bombarded by the evil empire of social media, pop-ups and clickbait, and endless time-sucking black holes of cascading links. All this data and inputs are so overwhelming, accompanied by an insane velocity of change and innovation. There is growing concern about the negative effects of this new environment of information overload causing depression, anxiety, and isolation. It's gotten so extreme that some people, stressed and depressed, are trying to impose a "digital Sabbath" on their endless scrolling by putting down their phones and logging off their laptops, while others are actually paying for apps that help them restrict their screen time. Paying to quit something you are also paying for (i.e., unlimited texts, call time, etc.). Crazy.

Not that long ago, we had many cultural and social rituals that gave us regular opportunities to pause: religious holidays, family events, birthdays, anniversaries, weddings, retirement parties, girls' weekends, annual family vacations, school sports matches, graduations—when was the last time you gave yourself permission to really be present for any of these? Or were you texting on your phone while your daughter drove down the soccer pitch heading for the goal? Were you doing a "fly by" to a family event, content with just "making an appearance"? My point here is that if we fail to take time to pause, we can never let the feeling of gratitude infuse us.

Pausing doesn't have to mean a month off or a semester-long sabbatical. In my high-pressure early days in finance, I would intentionally work late on Fridays, taking advantage of that time when everyone else had left the building. I'd spend a couple of hours finishing things that needed doing so Monday would not be hell. Then I treated myself to a delicious fresh salad from the Fairway Grocery and savored it on my sofa, while watching something fun on TV. That was my weekly pause. A time to relax, reset, and restore my sense of self and balance. These days, our practice is family movie night, with old-fashioned popcorn and plenty of phone-free hours spent together. Others find their pause in nature with a walk in the woods, a blanket on the beach, an evening of stargazing, or a bit of weeding in the garden. Even a micro moment when you just stop, and re-center can be the pause you need.

Expansive Gratitude

When the keynote speaker took the stage, his impressive size and obvious strength spoke to his career as a college championship wrestling coach. This guy was clearly a badass, so it was totally unexpected when he opened his remarks by talking about gratitude. What he wanted us to see was how powerful and formative thankfulness had been in his life and career. The things he was thankful for seemed boundless: his students, their parents, the competition, the refs, the spectators, his fellow coaches, the wins, and the losses. His gratitude recognized that all these elements contributed not just to his successes but to the person and leader they helped him become. Listening to this burly tough guy urge us to be grateful, well, it had an outsized effect on the audience because it was so surprising and obviously so true.

This is more than just one man's opinion. A variety of recent scientific experiments and research reports point to the many outcomes of being grateful. It can reduce inflammation, boost immunity, and even rewire the brain to promote positive emotions that contribute to a general sense of well-being. Doesn't that sound worth aiming for?

Let's be real. Sometimes your job doesn't go great; sometimes the markets don't love you. Stuff happens at home, at work, in the world. Being able to feel grateful despite the hard times is about playing the long game. It helps put into perspective your career, your relationships, and your overall mental, spiritual, and physical well-being. The human components of living your one life on this earth are really important. Important enough to be a large part of how you intentionally build a career that addresses all of these aspects of a full life.

Learning To Be Grateful

Like any new skill, establishing a solid foundation and practicing routinely is what builds mastery. One of the studies that tried to measure gratitude did so by asking participants a series of simple questions like these:

- What happened today that was good?
- What am I taking for granted that I can be thankful for?
- Which people in my life am I grateful for?
- What is the last book I read or movie, show, or social media clip I saw that I really appreciated, and why?
- What am I most looking forward to this week, month, and year, and why?
- What is the kindest thing someone has said or done lately?

The Hard Truth/ What Insiders Know

Gratitude is a personal and organizational source of restorative strength.

You'll notice that these questions look for the big and the small, the people and things, the immediate, the past, and the future. Learning to look all around us in space and time is a great way to build perspective. Answering these questions regularly can create a habit that serves to ground us and even get to know ourselves better. It can cause us to be more mindful of the things that feed us and, in the process, help us choose those over the things that deplete us.

These are all outcomes that benefit us as individuals, but they also have repercussions for our ability to lead. We all face work times when it's a really crappy day. We can demand that everyone on the team focus on the failure, but how would it change the dynamic if we found the one thing that was good? On an individual level, you can direct your emotions away from anger or frustration to something more positive. You can recognize that team members are helping you out and building each other up. You can be thankful for your people and their efforts, even when they fall short. That really, really helps motivate them in ways that can't be purchased. Making people feel the respect you have for them and the gratitude you have for their dedicated efforts makes a massive difference. Recognizing their contributions as part of your team, giving you great advice, being dependable, or being innovative helps solidify their motivation and desire to be on your team, in good times and in bad.

On a visit to a very high-performing group within a successful organization, I got to sit in on their Friday professional development workshop. Part of their end-of-the-week practice was to make time for peers to say thank you to each other for doing something that week, either personally or professionally, that made a difference. Their leader knew that peer gratitude was a marker of a great organization for its ability to build trust, collaboration, communication, and community.

One of my professors used to talk to us about gratitude. Inspired by his examples, I started writing thank-you notes pretty much every Saturday to clients, customers, and people I met along the way who had helped me. It's proven to be a great habit. It causes me to slow down and reflect on the week and the people I encountered. It helps me to be thankful for the big things and the little things. This act of pausing to be grateful feels like developing a muscle that is strong enough to fight off feeling down, or alone, or unsupported. It works for you and for the people you lead.

**Helpful Hack/
What Insiders Do**

They have a gratitude practice of their own that's personal.

They institutionalize a gratitude practice in their organizations.

TEN
Work and Life

This whole book has been about you, designed to be super focused on you and your career. I wrote it because, even though we may never meet, I care about your future, and I want to invest in you. That's why I'm willing to share these hard truths with you. And here is my last one: Living a life all about you is an empty life.

Part Three has been about encouraging you to go beyond finding a job or single-mindedly pursuing a career. That's hard work, but I urge you to do even more. The most gratifying lives sustain us while enabling us to be a part of something greater than ourselves.

Get Help to Give Help

In my personal and professional life, I know I have been extremely fortunate. So many generous and accomplished people have helped me as mentors, role models, and champions. I'd like to share a story that shows how sometimes your career unfolds like a relay race, where the baton gets passed from one influential person to another, enabling you to continue advancing toward your goals, and in the process, builds sustaining relationships that are deeper than any job or career.

When I was a young soldier based at Fort Hood, a massive training

The Hard Truth/ What Insiders Know

Your job doesn't love you back.

facility in Texas, I entered a highly competitive process to earn the position of Aide-de-Camp to an Army general. I'll never know how I won the role, but I did. Suddenly, I was on the inside, working closely with an accomplished leader who was responsible for thousands of men and women, military and civilian, across this huge enterprise. Every day, I witnessed how strategy unfolds, decisions get made, and crises get managed. I also saw how demanding such a leadership role is. We literally worked all the time.

The general approached his responsibilities with humility and a strong commitment to service. On more than one occasion, he reminded me that any of the dozens of colonels across the Army could have been made the rank of general. He attributed his own success to luck and hard work, believing he was no better than those he outranked. In fact, he was so committed to fairness and equality that, even though maintaining his uniforms was one of my jobs, he never asked me to take his clothes to the cleaners. And it wasn't until I insisted that he permitted me to open doors for him.

One of the numerous special events the general took part in was a golf tournament for the base. Although I had been a competitive athlete, golf was not my thing. I figured my "highest and best use" would be to drive his golf cart. "No way," the general said. "I need you to play golf so you can build relationships with the other members of the command. If they get to know you, they will tell you things they would never share with me. You will get a read on the morale and leadership of the other units on the base. These are things I need to know, so I can be a better leader. You have to learn to play golf." I signed up for lessons, and he made sure I was free every Wednesday at 4 PM—or in Army language 1600—even though that meant I showed up to play in combat boots, not your standard golf attire. On some weekends, he invited me to join him and his wife to play a few holes after the course was closed. It helped my game, but mostly it was fun to get to know him off duty.

By tournament time, I wish I could tell you that I had become a good golfer, but that would be a big stretch. I did not play golf well, but I did know the rules. And one solid piece of advice the general gave me was, "If you don't know how to play, at least play fast."

Being willing to learn, being open to advice, and being trusted to build relationships with senior officers were all career accelerants. When I was later asked to take part in a West Point alumni tournament, I accepted and lucked out to have an amazing golfer as my partner. The relationships that I formed that day opened more doors, and over time, I kept getting more opportunities for career development and, in the end, career advancement. From being a volunteer for a silent auction to benefit the alumni association, to becoming a board member of the association, to taking part in a leadership conference where I met someone who went on to champion my efforts to serve on the board of a publicly traded company, all could be traced back to not taking the easy way out by driving the golf cart.

Ultimately, it didn't matter that my golf game wasn't much. The people in this story were of service to me. I came to really care about them and to be grateful for their mentorship, advice, and belief in me. When I reflect on this journey, what stands out is how great a difference it makes to know the rules in the large sense, to be open to mentors and coaches to teach you, to be willing to get help and make the extra effort. I felt the power of relationships as a kind of pulley system—people who care about you will literally pull you up. You have to come dressed and ready to play, even if that means wearing combat boots on the green.

These things don't happen if you're looking to do less or are unwilling to do things differently. And once you've benefitted from the kindness of others, you can find purpose in bringing other people along. These people became a treasured part of the fabric of my life. Being of service in this way, as a giver and as a receiver, is so much bigger than any career move because it connects you to the human experience.

Being of Service

I worked with an executive once who had recently been promoted to a highly visible leadership role. Every meeting after his big promotion, he would mention "my role." It became so extreme that team members would tally up his mention of "my role" during meetings because that was all they were listening for. All he could talk about was himself. This person was so obviously me-centered that it started to repel even the people who had helped him get to the top.

In contrast, I've also worked for a leader who was all about the "we." She constantly sent notes to the senior management calling attention to team wins. She described how each person contributed to the win, from the executive assistant to the researcher to the team leaders. She inspired others and attracted talented people to her team. Her inclusive approach to leadership created the sort of work environment that lights up others and, in turn, leads to greater success.

Time and time again, watching managers at various levels and in different industries, I've seen the same dynamic unfold. When you live to serve others, you unlock something in your own life that connects you with the humans that came before you and the humans that come after you.

A lot of people talk about management skills and leadership roles, offering advice about how to do them. They tend to promote certain practices and attitudes, advocating for things like holding feedback sessions, developing communication plans, adopting a strategic mindset, and committing to agility. All these are really important. But the very most important mindset is service. There is no bigger joy than to be of service to others. Many people have said this, and it's true: The more you give, the more you get.

If you wake up in the morning, thinking about your teammates, or your clients and customers, about others and not yourself, you not only have what it takes to be a manager, you have what it takes to be a leader. You will be a leader at home with your family, with your neighbors, and with your company. If all you care about is yourself and getting ahead, people smell it like the warning scent of a feral animal. People will stay away.

I've been talking about being of service as a mindset at work, but it's a way of being that can carry into every aspect of your life. I saw this early on in my life because my mother was a role model of selflessness and generosity. For forty years, she volunteered to clean our church. She was the one who drove me to 5 AM swim practice, then chauffeured me all over the state for meets on the weekends. Ours was a modest household, but there was always enough to help someone else who was having a rough time. My mom was like a one-person lasagna factory, always ready with a tray to share. Even now in her eighties, she takes the "old" ladies out for lunch and goes to the personal care home to visit the residents. Especially in small towns, but even in urban neighborhoods, people like my mom are the ones who make a family and make communities into families too. Their generosity, kindness, and willingness to be of service, whether as volunteer firefighters, Little League coaches, school bake sale contributors, or election poll volunteers, form the lifeblood and the steel girders of healthy, vibrant, connected communities. Just the sort of places where we want to live and raise our families.

Your Three-Legged Stool

This chapter opened with the hard truth that no matter what, your job does not love you back. If you want to find balance and fulfillment, it's helpful to think about your life as a three-legged stool. One leg is your job that earns you the money you need to live and ideally provides some joy in your career. The second leg is your personal need for purpose, wellness, spirituality, and resilience. The third represents your enriching relationships with your spouse or partner, deep friendships, and your larger community.

You have to spend time on all of these relationships. Work and career take time. When you decide to go nonstop, working all the time, you get a payoff in the form of career advancement. I'm calling out that time and effort are also what you have to invest in relationships. At work, we build relationships and friendships that are sometimes deep and life-long. But it is important to know that these relationships are often tied to a particular workplace. People move on, retire, relocate to a new state, etc. I don't want you to find yourself having invested all the eggs in the work basket only to feel alone when that basket gets dropped or breaks.

The investment that you make in your career comes at a price: you can't be at drinks with your future spouse and at your desk working on an exciting project. The career payoff means time away from your friends and family. Where you invest time, you see results.

Don't wait to invest time and energy into your loved ones, your family, your adopted family, and your friends. Cultivate deep relationships where you find them, with neighbors, your church traveling choir, synagogue, or community gardeners. Like a garden, you need to tend to these relationships, or they will not be there when the project is over, when the client is mad at you, or even when you retire.

Early on in life, all these legs may be slender and barely formed. But if you bring awareness and commitment to strengthening each leg over time, like the way a tree adds rings year over year, your three-legged stool grows sturdier and more stable. You gain experience and expertise in your career. You practice self-care and tend to your health. You build and nurture meaningful connections with other people. As we mature, our sense of self and competence grows, as does our ability to be in right relationship with ourselves and others. This evolution is based on developing not our IQ but our EQ, our emotional quotient or intelligence that results from humbly embracing all the lessons learned from our failures and successes. A life without each of these three legs is as unstable and uneven as an unfinished stool.

It has been a privilege to be working at the very center of executive recruiting across national and international enterprises and operating in a wide variety of industries. I have seen first-hand, literally in the privacy behind closed doors, how companies big and small, located in densely populated global cities or tucked away in rural America, attract and retain the leaders that propel them to success. Through meeting and interacting with highly accomplished board members and CEOs, I have enjoyed the most incredible opportunity to learn from the very best.

> **Helpful Hack/**
> **What Insiders Do**
>
> They know the rules and even when they are not the most expert, they show up dressed and ready to play.
>
> They think of serving others before themselves.
>
> They invest in their family and relationships as much as their career.

This has been the gift of my career and an inspiration in my life. I'm lucky that many of these folks have become my friends. One throughline that I see in each and every one of the very best of these people and their companies is their consistent, authentic commitment to be in service to others at work, at home, and in their respective communities. Their willingness to serve translates to passion. These leaders and the companies they lead not only unlock their own potential, but they also unleash excellence in everyone around them.

Unleash yourself in service to others. You will find joy and a true connection to the world.

Acknowledgments

Thank you to my husband, Tony, and our kids for inspiring me to write something that captures some of my professional lessons learned. Thank you for listening, reading, and joking with me. Thank you to the girls and young women in my life: I thought about you reading this in a moment that you need to hear some hard truths, or just maybe, read it before you need it. This is not *War and Peace*, right? Thank you to my parents, you gave me a foundation of love and opportunity. I love you.

Thank you to my communities: our families, church, hometown, West Point, West Point Women, HKS, HBS, all my classmates and the alumnae and alumni of these great institutions; my mom networks, the swim teams, triathlon clubs, veterans, and caregivers. I'm lucky to have you—a crazy mix of people that are here in this rural county, in a business metropolis, or somewhere halfway across the world. Wherever you are, thank you for your friendship, whether I see you once a week or once a decade. A special call out to Fran, Dena, Sara, Divina, Jim, and Marilyn, who, in this season, provided me with unique support as this book launched out the door. You are an example of selfless service, hard work, teamwork, and love. I learn from you every day and admire you. I'm grateful to you.

And thank you to Major General John Schofield and Admiral Hyman G. Rickover. I never met you, but your ideas and words have inspired me, specifically Schofield's Definition of Discipline and Admiral Rickover's Morgenthau Memorial Lecture in 1982. West Pointers will know of Schofield's message, and it is easy to Google. But Rickover's thoughts on careers are harder to find. About a year after I joined Korn Ferry, I came across his quote in *The Wall Street Journal*. It rang as clear and true as a church bell to me. I taped it into the back cover of my notebook. It still speaks to me now: "But having a vocation means more than punching a time clock. It means guarding against banality, ineptitude, incompetence, and mediocrity. A man should strive to become a locus of excellence." I have found a miracle, and it is something like love!